THE CURE-ALL

It isn't money.

It isn't power.

It isn't sex.

It's not love, religion, education, technology or democracy.

But there is one simple solution to the many complex problems of life.

It's The Cure-All, and from this book you'll learn how and why it can't miss!

THE CURE-ALL

by John Tydings

Midnight Marquee Press, Inc.
Baltimore, Maryland, USA

Copyright © 1991 Original Edition by John Tydings
Copyright © 2012 Revised Edition by John Tydings
Interior layout: Gary J. Svehla
Cover design: Susan Svehla
Copy editor: Linda J. Walter

Reprinted by Midnight Marquee Press, Inc.
First printing by It's Life and Life Only Publications, September 1993

Midnight Marquee Press, Inc., Gary J. Svehla and A. Susan Svehla do not assume any responsibility for the accuracy, completeness, topicality or quality of the information in this book. All views expressed or material contained within are the sole responsibility of the author.

Without limiting the rights under copyright reserved above, no part of this publication may be reproduced, stored in or introduced into a retrieval system, or transmitted, in any form, or by any means (electronic, mechanical, photocopying, recording or otherwise), without the prior written permission of the copyright owner or the publishers of the book.

ISBN 13: 978-1-936168-26-2
Library of Congress Catalog Card Number 2012938168
Manufactured in the United States of America

First Revised Printing by Midnight Marquee Press, Inc., May 2012

Dedication

To everybody who ever searched for a cure-all but couldn't find one before.

Quotations found throughout the text are in the public domain, with the exception of "If I Were a Rich Man" from *Fiddler on the Roof*, written by Jerry Bock and Sheldon Harnick.

The Cure-All is a philosophical treatise—**not** a how-to manual. It is intended to stimulate thought and discussion among mentally competent adults rather than to advocate a particular course of action for anyone. Neither the publisher nor the author can assume responsibility for any personal conclusions that might be drawn by the reader. Let everyone decide for oneself.

Table of Contents

Introduction: Fear and Desire — 8

Chapter 1: Ignorance and Knowledge — 10

Chapter 2: Pain and Pleasure — 35

Chapter 3: Hate and Love — 40

Chapter 4: Evil and Good — 44

Chapter 5: Necessity and Freedom — 49

Chapter 6: Poverty and Wealth — 65

Chapter 7: War and Peace — 91

Chapter 8: Despair and Faith — 97

Conclusion: The Problem and the Solution — 117

Postscript — 139

Introduction: Fear and Desire

There are just two reasons for doing anything: desire and fear. We act in order to get what we want or to avoid getting what we don't want. Our efforts would always succeed if it weren't for the problems that beset us constantly.

Everyone has problems. A problem is anything that thwarts our desires or excites our fears. It prevents us from getting what we want or from avoiding what we don't want.

Every action that we take is an attempt to solve some problem. No matter what we try to do, we always encounter some resistance to our effort. And whether that resistance is small or large, it must be overcome before we can solve the problem and thereby satisfy our desire or allay our fear.

Needs may be regarded as overpowering desires or as the means to their fulfillment. If we want something badly enough, then we need it in order to be happy (and everyone wants to be happy). Few of us relish the prospect of surgery; but, when we are ill, we may feel that we have to undergo a painful operation if that is our only chance of regaining the health we covet. Whether or not we enjoy eating, we require food if we desire life; we need the means to existence only if we want to exist. There are no needs without desires.

Our problems are endless because our desires and fears are endless. The satisfaction of one desire only gives birth to a new desire. Air is our first desire, followed (in no particular order) by water, food, sleep, clothing, shelter and sex. Having provided for our bodies, we proceed to satisfy the so-called higher needs: those for security, love, status, power, *ad infinitum*. Equally infinite are the fears of not satisfying those desires, namely, the fears of suffocation, dehydration, starvation, insomnia, exposure, homelessness, frustration, insecurity, loneliness, inferiority, vulnerability and so forth.

Society is formed for the purpose of solving those problems that we cannot solve on our own. Different institutions of society are intended to solve different problems: business, industry, agriculture and government are supposed to address our lower needs while churches, schools and family life take care of the higher ones. To one extent or another, these institutions perform the functions for which they were designed.

Still, the problems remain. In fact, they keep growing in both number and complexity. Why?

One reason, as we saw before, is that the solution of every specific problem gives rise to another problem. If you have air, then you need water; if you have water, then you need food; and so on, through the limited lower needs into the unlimited higher ones. But there's more to it than this.

Our ancestors founded human society to solve problems that they couldn't solve by their individual efforts. In so doing, they created a whole new set of problems. Each member of society is a unique person with his own desires. In order to secure the cooperation of his fellow members, he must curb such desires. Such self-denial causes problems for the individual. Society itself experiences difficulties in maintaining itself and its institutions against the competing claims of other societies and even those of its own members. In a word, society entails compromise. (When you win, you're happy; when you lose, your opponent is happy; but when you compromise, no one is happy.)

Up to a point, society requires an increasing population to serve as workers, consumers and defenders. But the more people in society, the more problems there are bound to be, the more competing desires to be compromised and the more conflicts to be resolved.

The ultimate dream of both individuals and societies is to have their problems solved once and for all. Specific solutions to specific problems, as we have seen, only engender new problems; so the only permanent solution must be a cure-all, a solution to end all solutions and thus all problems.

From time immemorial, dreamers have sought a cure-all, but usually in the wrong places. Among the concrete solutions thought to be final have been money, power and sensual gratification; the more abstract solutions have included education, morality, technology and the worship of God and/or country. All of these attempts have failed, as evidenced by the misery that continues to prevail throughout the world. Optimists go on making the same attempts, while pessimists despair of ever finding a cure-all; they are both wrong.

The cure-all exists. It has always existed, and it always will. We can find it, and we shall.

To realize what the cure-all is, we must first understand what it is not. Accordingly, we will examine some of life's most common problems (specifically, ignorance, pain, hate, evil, necessity, poverty, war and despair) and see why none of their standard solutions (knowledge, pleasure, love, good, freedom, wealth, peace and religious faith) can be what we're looking for. When no more blind alleys are left to enter, we shall find the road that leads to the cure-all.

The best way to get something done is to begin. So, let's begin.

Chapter 1: Ignorance and Knowledge

Before we can arrive at any final answers, we need to ask ourselves some basic questions. What can we know? How do we know it? Of what can we be certain?

At least we can be sure of one thing: We know what we perceive. And we perceive sights, sounds, odors, flavors and textures by means of our five senses. For example, we may see, smell, taste and touch an apple after hearing the sound it makes falling from a tree. When you and I both perceive the same apple, we are sensing something in common (and thereby displaying "common sense").

But this is not all that we perceive: It is just the beginning. Our memory provides the link between our concrete sensations and our abstract conceptions. Remembering that the apple we ate was red, round, sweet and firm, we get an idea of "redness," "roundness," "sweetness" and "firmness"; we form simple concepts like these by noting the characteristics exhibited by the objects of our perception. If we eat enough fruits like the first one, then we will know what an "apple" is without having to see, smell, taste or touch it beforehand. By associating the simple concepts of redness, roundness, sweetness and firmness in our minds, we produce the complex concept of an apple (or at least one variety of it).

Complex concepts, then, are derived by relating simple concepts to one another and by combining the qualities shared by a number of different objects into the same mental category. ("If you've seen one, you've seen them all.") The formation of concepts, whether simple or complex, is a process of abstracting from particular sensations to general ideas.

A sensation is the first type of perception, but not the last. As we have seen, we perceive simple and complex concepts that we have derived from our own sensations by reflecting upon those sensations. (A reflection is a mental perception of a sensory perception or of another mental perception.) We perceive memories and dreams, relate sensations and concepts to one another and to each other in the thought process, and we make judgments based on those sensations and concepts. But in everything we do, we perceive either directly (in the case of sensation) or indirectly (in the case of reflection, which is the perception of perception[s]).

To repeat, there are two kinds of perceptions: sensations and reflections. Sensations are the direct, immediate perceptions of our physical senses, while reflections are perceptions of sensations and all other perceptions. A perceiving subject may reflect upon a sensation or upon another reflection. Sensations, then, are primary perceptions; reflections can be secondary, tertiary and so on.

One of the first concepts that we derive from our sensory experience is that of existence itself, because the objects of our perception exist for our consciousness. The primal concept of existence can be defined as the perception of an object by a subject, the subject being that which perceives and the object being that which is perceived. Without at least one subject and one object in the world, nothing can exist.

You are the subject; this book and everything else in the world that you perceive are your objects. At the same time, you are an object for yourself because you can perceive your own body by means of your five senses. You can perceive your own mind by reflecting upon it, that is, by perceiving through memory, dreaming, thought and judgment.

Your self, then, is both a subject and an object. Everything other than you is merely your object. It exists for you only if you perceive it. If you stop perceiving the other, then–for all you know–it may no longer exist at all. You can feel *for* another person, but you can never feel *with* him.

The self and the other are differentiated by sensation and reflection. Pain and pleasure, two qualities of our sensory perceptions, are felt directly only by oneself. Their experience by another person or thing may be inferred by the self from the other's cries, gestures or expressions—but never known directly.

The second way in which the self discriminates between itself and the other is by employing the concept of causality, or the assumption that everything is produced by a prior cause. Normally, the self can cause its body to move by willing it to do so from the inside; in contrast, the self can move the other only by acting upon it from the outside. The self is under its own direct control, while the other is at best under the indirect control of the self.

Human beings take special pride in the form of reflection that they believe sets them apart from the so-called lower animals, namely, their reason. While many other animals are able to draw conclusions based on their prior perceptions, they apparently cannot relate as many concepts to one another as most people can. A human's thought processes are probably more complex than those of other animals, and his capacity to produce changes in himself and his world are undeniably greater. If intelligence is the ability to solve problems, then, for all we know, man is the highest animal on Earth. But since he may also be able to create more problems than any other animal, we will refrain from calling him the best.

By means of his reason, man compiles an impressive list of achievements. First he conceives a theory, then puts it into practice. While other animals may or may not harbor the same aesthetic sensibility as man, they lack his power to express that vision as clearly in the tangible form of art. (Few serious art critics would lump the finger paintings of a chimp at the zoo in the same category as Leonardo da Vinci's *Mona Lisa*.) Nonhuman animals are likewise incapable of analyzing themselves and their environments as man does in his social and natural sciences. But the most significant difference between the lower animals and the highest animal is that he alone is able to make practical applications of his theories, with far-reaching consequences for himself and everything around him.

The first fruit of man's reason is his language. He contrives a verbal and/or written symbol for each class of objects that he and his fellows sense in common. In so doing, he comes to possess an effective tool for promoting communication and joint effort. So important is this device to man that he tries to polish and preserve it by devising grammar, a set of rules and regulations intended to govern the use of language.

Just as grammar is man's attempt to impose law and order upon language, so does logic represent his attempt to legislate the thought process at work behind language. While grammarians tell us how we should speak and write, logicians tell us how we should think. If we do not attack a problem logically, then we are guilty of "incorrect" thinking, even if we come up with the right solution. Logic may be viewed as the pride of reason.

Deduction is that method of logic that proceeds from general concepts to specific cases. If the premises of an argument are accepted on authority, then the proper conclusion that can be drawn from them follows logically. For instance:

> All apples are red.
> The Golden Delicious is an apple.
> Therefore, the Golden Delicious is red.

The above is an example of a valid argument and correct reasoning; the prior assumptions lead necessarily to the conclusion. Unfortunately, the conclusion is false because the major premise that all apples are red is untrue. On the other hand, a conclusion may be true while the argument is invalid.

> All apples are red.
> The Golden Delicious is an apple.
> Therefore, the Golden Delicious is yellow.

Despite the fact that the Golden Delicious apple is yellow (at least until it rots), the above argument is incorrect because the conclusion does not follow from the major premise that we were expected to accept on authority.

Nobody who knows anything about apples would dare to suggest that all of them are red. It is nevertheless risky to give our unquestioning credence to authority—whatever the topic may be. For many centuries, some learned astronomers believed that the Earth was located at the center of the universe. Those in authority may be mistaken or even dishonest. If we are going to take their assumptions for granted, we might at least inquire as to how they arrived at them. The point is that deduction rests upon the foundation of authority, and there is no reasoning with the person who demands a reason for everything.

Deductive logic lends itself admirably to arithmetic, geometry and other branches of mathematics. In the following argument

> The sum of two pairs always equals four.
> Two plus two is the sum of two pairs.
> Therefore, two plus two equals four.

the premises entail the conclusion. This is always the case with valid deductions because their conclusions merely restate in particular what their premises have asserted in general. Similarly, the geometric theorem given below

> If all sides of a quadrilateral are equal and parallel, then that quadrilateral is a square.

illustrates the necessity by which a correct conclusion follows from a premise. Anything that one can truly say about a square is summed up in the concept's own definition. If we assume the premises of deductive arguments to be true, then we must believe that their valid conclusions are also true.

We have no trouble taking the assumptions of mathematicians on authority, for they in fact are the authors of their own discipline. They created, rather than discovered, math. They defined sums and products and squares and circles and, having done so, determined the properties of their creations once and for all. Forevermore, a round figure bounded by a line whose every point is equidistant from its internal center shall be a perfect circle. Sadly, there is no such thing as a perfect circle except in geometry textbooks or the minds of mathematicians, and we must look further if we are to acquire knowledge of the real world.

Some seekers of truth believe they have already found the way—by traveling in a direction that is the exact opposite of the path followed by practitioners of deductive reasoning. They employ the inductive method of logic, a process by which universal principles are derived from particular observations. Instead of taking for granted the pronouncement of some dubious authority that all apples are red, they would examine many different apples and discover that these fruits can be red, green, yellow, brown and various shades of these same colors. If the investigators personally inspected a million apples from all over the world, they might draw the conclusion that no apple is blue. Such a conclusion is probably true—but not necessarily. No logical contradiction is involved in the conception of a blue apple; moreover, it would be impossible to perceive every apple in the world, and it is always possible for a blue apple to exist somewhere, as yet unnoticed. An inference from induction can never be proven, but it can be refuted when new evidence comes to light.

Scientists use a mixture of induction, trial and error and refined common sense to conduct their research. Reflection upon sensory perceptions leads to the formulation of general concepts by this method. After making a preliminary assumption about the object he is studying, the scientist performs an experiment and repeats it again and again in order to verify the results. He analyzes his numerous observations and, in the process, comes to accept or reject his initial hypothesis. If he feels that his research is important enough, he may publish his findings so that other investigators in the same field can test the results. But no matter how many times the scientist and his colleagues reach the same conclusion, there is no guarantee that the scientific theory established thereby will stand the test of time.

The scientific community believed that an imaginary substance called "phlogiston" produced fire—until Joseph Priestly discovered oxygen in 1774. Even Priestly continued to believe in phlogiston until Antoine Lavoisier demonstrated in the same year that burning resulted from the rapid combination of oxygen with a combustible material. A trillion experiments cannot prove the truth of a theory, but it takes only one to disprove it.

Once established, a scientific theory will enjoy a high degree of probability as long as it provides the best possible explanation for the facts as we know them. It will lose its currency when someone thinks of a better theory or when new facts contradict old beliefs. The Ptolemaic system, according to which Earth occupies the fixed center of the universe, worked quite well until discoveries in geography and astronomy forced people to accept the heliocentric view of Copernicus. For more than two centuries, Sir Isaac Newton's theory of gravitation dominated physics, but it left just enough questions unanswered to enable Albert Einstein's theory of relativity to supplant it as the most comprehensive worldview yet. Einstein himself modified his own theory to accommodate the insights of Bernhard Riemann, and further developments (such as string theory) may someday consign relativity to the scrapheap of scientific history.

The science of human nature is even less certain than the science of nature at large. Unlike the chemist in his laboratory, the psychologist, sociologist, anthropologist, economist, historian or political scientist cannot perform experiments under rigidly controlled conditions. They must usually confine themselves to observing people from a distance and inferring the causes of human behavior from many possible alternatives. Their inability to regulate independent variables often fosters, in each discipline, a number of competing theories to explain the same phenomenon. (Widely divergent theories tend to prevail consecutively in natural science–and concurrently in social science.)

One sociologist, for example, might tell you that heredity is the cause of crime, while another one may claim that environment is responsible. Each could undoubtedly marshal a vast array of statistics to prove his own point. Your choice between the two viewpoints would be largely a matter of personal preference.

Like all induction, the scientific method is designed to establish the probability of a theory, and it is only as reliable as the current information on which it is based. New evidence may render the theory more or less probable.

Similarly, deductive logic determines the validity of an argument, whose conclusion is only as true as its underlying assumption. This assumption, in turn, must be accepted on authority—and authority is questionable. Furthermore, a deductive argument commonly begs the question by assuming (or even defining) in its premise what it states in its conclusion. ("If a round, plane figure is enclosed by a line whose every point is equally distant from its center, then the figure is a circle.")

All inductive reasoning is tentative, and all deductive reasoning is circular. Logic is an approach to truth, but it is not truth itself.

In our quest for knowledge, we have returned to the point from which we started. We know for certain that we perceive things—sensations and reflections, to be exact, but we are not always so sure what to make of them.

Q. If a tree falls in a forest where there is no person or other animal to hear it, or any device to record it, would it make a sound?
A. No.

A sound is a perception, a sensation excited by mechanical disturbances (known as "sound waves") vibrating through a medium (such as air) to the ear of a conscious being (that is, a human or other animal). The falling tree would probably produce vibrations, but they would fail to stimulate the auditory apparatus of a conscious being if no such being were within earshot. In short, the tree would make sound waves but no sound. Since hearing is only one form of sensation and sensation just one type of perception, another question arises—

Q. Would a tree continue to exist in the forest if no conscious being were there to perceive it?
A. No.

If the falling tree made no sounds in the deserted forest, then neither would it produce any other sensations. It would not have any shape or color because there would be no one around to see the light reflected from its surface. It would possess no texture because no one would touch its bark. It would be devoid of tastes and odors, as no creature would eat its leaves, drink its sap or smell its aroma. Whether it fell or remained standing, the tree would not exist for anyone or anything.

Existence, as we noted earlier, is the perception of an object by a subject. Without a subject, there can be no object. Without a conscious being to perceive it, nothing can exist as the object of that being's perception.

Yet common sense tells us that things continue to exist even if we stop perceiving them. After all, we might still be able to find our initials on the same tree into which we carved them as children—even if we haven't seen this tree for the last 30 years.

The problem with common sense is that it's too often common and too seldom sensible. Please remember that, for thousands of years, most people believed that the Earth was flat and stationary. If it were round or mobile, they argued, then we'd all fall off! Anyone who thought otherwise obviously lacked common sense. And the fact is that this "flat-earth" assumption worked quite well for humankind until travel and exploration became global in scope.

Nonetheless, whenever we find ourselves agreeing with the majority, it might be time to reconsider our position. Common sense may serve all practical purposes and still be in error. To proceed, we must look at things in a very uncommon way.

It is necessary to draw a sharp line between existence and Being. To exist is to be the object of a subject, the perception of a perceiver, the content of a consciousness. To be is to be, regardless of who perceives, what is perceived or anything else. Existence, then, is relative to perception, while Being is absolute, that is, relative to nothing.

Our tree in the forest would cease to exist for us if we stopped perceiving it, but it would probably continue to be as long as it had a being of its own (i.e., until it was physically destroyed). We can never be sure of how permanent the tree would be in the absence of our perception, for perception is our only means of verifying its permanence. But when we view the tree again after 30 years, we recognize our initials and infer that this is the same tree we knew so long ago. It has been here since we last perceived it, even though we have not directly perceived it again until now—and in spite of the fact that, for the last three decades, it has ceased to exist for us except perhaps in our memories (as a reflection of our past sensations).

Being is nothing, but everything comes from it. It is no thing, neither a subject to perceive nor an object to be perceived. As the One and Only, it does not exist in its pure state—though it is the ground and the source of existence. In the state of nonexistence, Being is at One with Itself.

Existence is the other state of Being. It divides the One into many, splitting Being into beings and nothing into things. These things we call subject and object, and they are the necessary conditions of existence. Without them, there would be no world.

The two states of existence are life and non-life. For the sake of convenience, we will adopt a standard scientific definition of life as the ability of an object to grow, reproduce, metabolize nutrients and respond to stimuli. Anything unable to perform such functions would fall into the category of non-life (or "death").

Every conscious being is alive, but not every live being is conscious. Accordingly, the two states of life are consciousness and unconsciousness. Only those life forms with sufficiently developed nervous systems are capable of becoming conscious subjects, while all of the others are just potential objects like the non-life forms.

The word "exist" derives from a Latin word which means to "stand out" or to "come forth," and this original meaning is quite appropriate. To exist, indeed, is to stand out from Being and to come forth from it. When you look at a tree in the forest and focus upon it, you cause that tree to stand out from the background of the forest. In like manner, any conscious subject causes the object of its perception to stand out from the ground of its Being. Existence is to Being as a figure to its ground.

As the substratum of existence, Being underlies everything—each and every thing. The world exists while Being subsists. The world stands out from Being as Being stands under the world.

To create something is to bring it into being or to cause it to come into existence. Being creates the world by bringing it into being. A conscious being creates the world by bringing it out of Being; that is, a subject causes the world to come forth from pure Being into existence. Being creates the world by conceiving it, while a subject creates its own part of the world by perceiving it. Without Being itself, the world could not have begun. Without a conscious being, it could not continue.

The fundamental relationship between existence and Being can be understood in terms of an analogy. An eye might see many things, but the most it could ever see of itself is its own reflection in a mirror of some sort. Let the eye represent Being and the mirror represent the world of objects in which Being sees itself in its various aspects. A window will stand for the individual subject through which a Being views the world. And a mirror in which Being sees reflections of itself will symbolize the world. The more windows there are, the more subjective viewpoints Being will have to see the world from different angles. Being's view of itself is limited by the (window) frame of reference of the subject, which sees itself as an object in the world by reflecting on its own perceptions. Being itself is not a subject, for the subject is one of the two things that comprise existence. (The other is the object.) All things come from Being, but Being itself is nothing and therefore comes from nothing. (Please refer to figures 1a and 1b.)

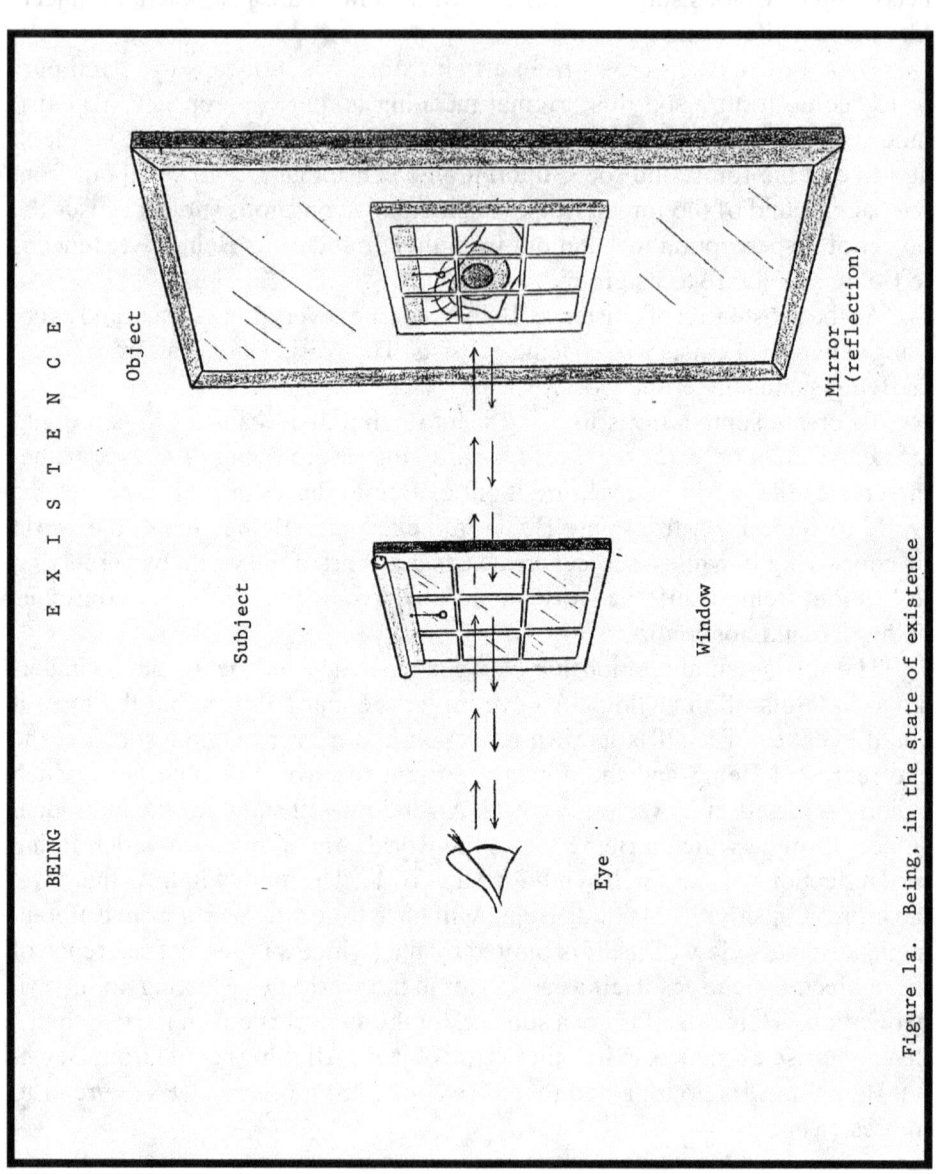

Figure 1a. Being, in the state of existence

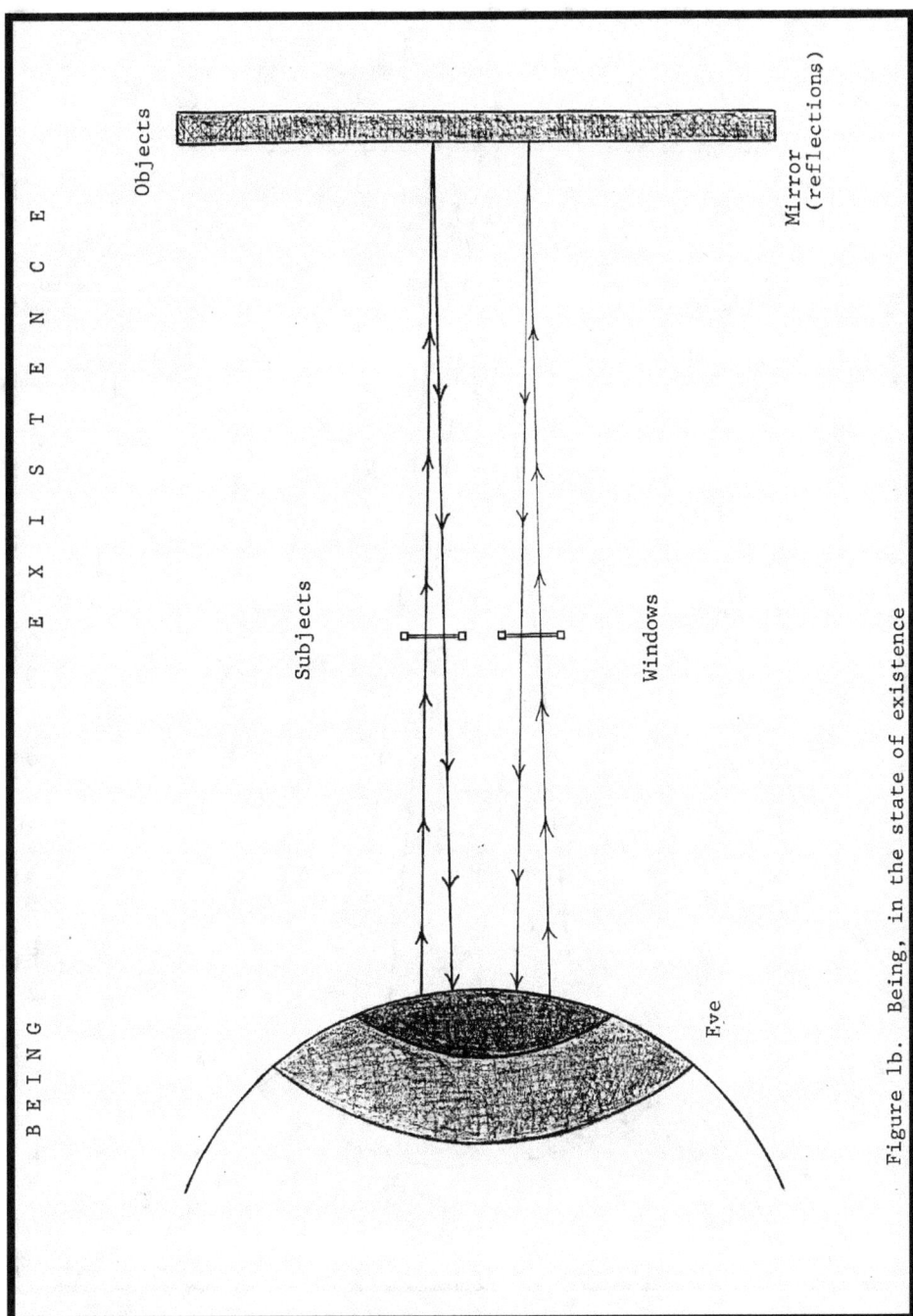

Figure 1b. Being, in the state of existence

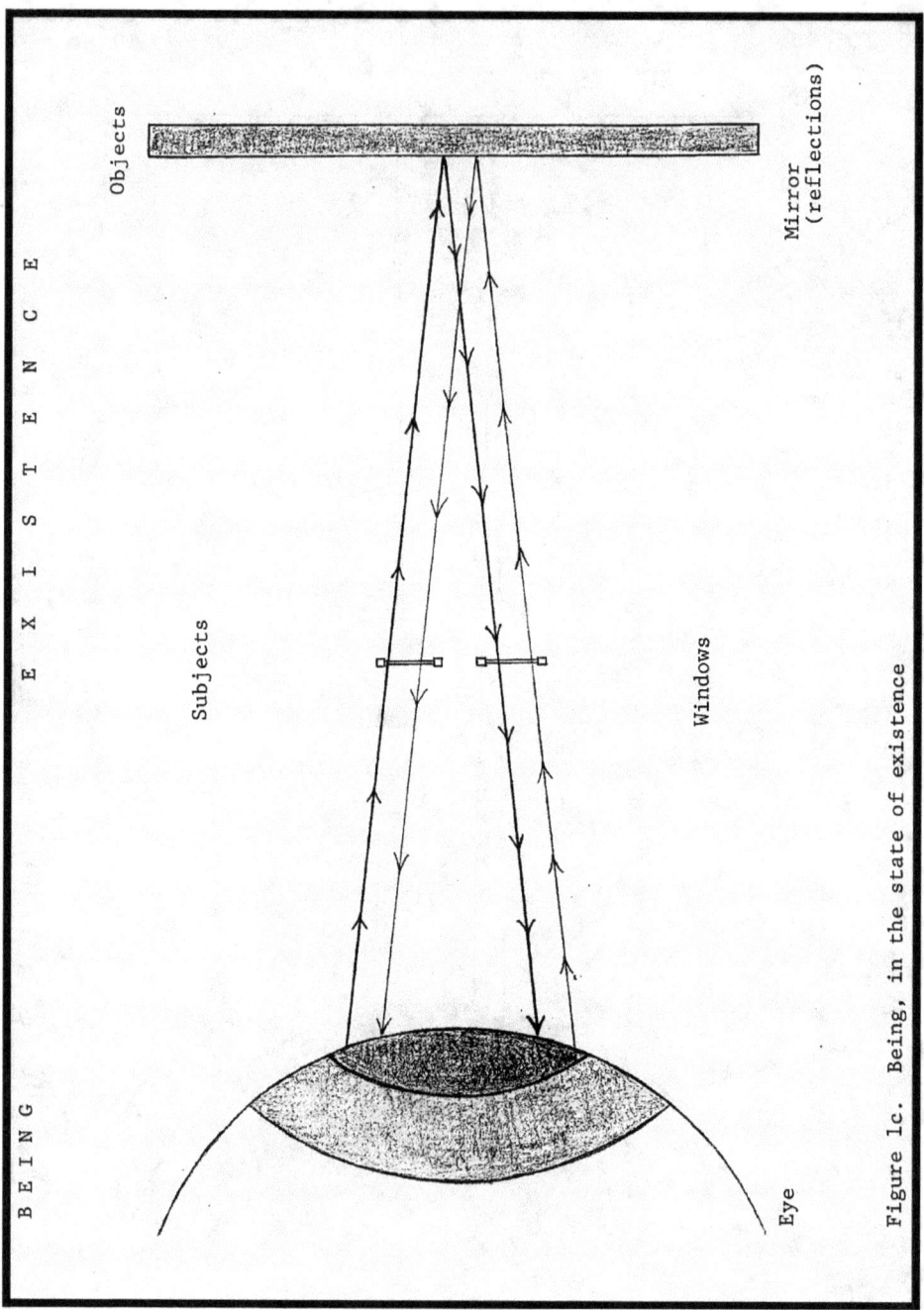

Figure 1c. Being, in the state of existence

As indicated by the preceding figure (1c; left), subjects do not perceive each other directly. Instead, they see one another as objects reflected in the world. No subject ever sees another subject; it sees only the objectified expressions of another subjective consciousness. You may see another person's body, but you can never see his mind. You hear words and see gestures while the actual thoughts and feelings behind them remain hidden from you. This radical opacity of one human being to another is what makes misunderstanding and deceit possible.

The analogy and accompanying illustrations are useful as long as they are not taken too literally. In its state of existence, Being is not distinct from subject or object, as it would appear to be in figures 1a, 1b and 1c; instead, subjects and objects are part of existent Being, and the windows and mirrors may be regarded as projections of the eye. Electromagnetic light radiates from a natural or man-made source before it strikes an earthly organism's eye directly or is reflected from some other surface. In the two diagrams, however, the light emanates from Being's eye itself because, ultimately, everything comes from Being itself. Being is All in all.

As the division of the One into the many, existence is essentially a process of disintegration. The Whole is broken into parts. Where there was only Being, there is now a multitude of beings. Each being is a subject or object or both.

Being in the state of nonexistence is pure Being itself, and Being is nothing. As such, it is infinitely and eternally empty. In the state of existence, the emptiness of Being is perceived as space and time.

Space is the infinite void of the One Being, which existence tries to fill with many finite beings. Although it is not sensed directly by the subject, it is conceived as an infinite number of points constituting the precondition of sensory objects. Space makes possible the coexistence of two or more objects at the same time as well as the change in position of a single object over a period of time.

Time is the eternal void of the One Being, which existence tries to fill with many mutable beings. The change in the forms, positions and/or compositions of perceived objects is how the subject experiences time. The present is the way in which those objects appear at the moment one perceives them directly. The past is the way in which one remembers them from a prior perception, and the future is the way in which one expects to perceive them. Only the present moment exists as an object of immediate perception, but the past lingers in the subject's memory while the future looms in one's imagination as a projection from the past and present experiences. If the sun rose yesterday and today, then it will probably rise again tomorrow.

Like everything else in the existing world, time and space are relative. The "here and now" is any point in space occupied by the subject at the present moment. Any other place and time would be "there and then." Distance is the amount of space between any two points perceived by the subject (who himself occupies a particular point in space from which he may view other points). Time is measured by comparing the successive positions of one object (like the Earth) with those of another object (like the moon or sun) or else by calculating the relative proportions of two parts (say, uranium and lead) of the same object (such as a rock).

Motion and speed are determined in a similar fashion. A passenger on a moving train feels motionless as he sees the countryside rush past the window. A switchman on a platform watches the train hurtle by at 100 miles an hour and imagines that he himself is standing still—while the planet under his feet rotates at a speed of 1,000 miles per hour! ("Speed equals distance divided by time.") Everything is relative to the subject's viewpoint, and together, time and space constitute the relationship of things in the world.

Anything that takes up space is matter, which composes the physical objects in the world. One or more of a subject's five senses can perceive material objects. Matter displays inertia, the tendency of an object in motion to stay in motion or of an object at rest to stay at rest unless acted upon by some force. In other words, matter offers resistance to change.

Energy, in contrast to matter, is the capacity for change itself. Put simply, energy is the ability to do work, to apply a force through a distance. In performing work, energy is transferred from one object to another in the direction of the applied force and against whatever resistance may be offered by matter.

Energy can become potential, kinetic, thermal, mechanical, electrical, magnetic or nuclear. It is even able to overcome the inertia of matter, thereby changing matter from a state of rest to one of motion and vice-versa, or from a solid to a liquid to a gas to a plasma in any desired order. As illustrated by the products of chemical reactions, energy can alter the form and rearrange the content of matter.

Energy causes change while matter resists it. Energy acts; matter is acted upon. Since these two phenomena are the exact opposites of each other, matter may be viewed as the mirror image of energy. This contrariety of energy and matter is ironic, since the two are interchangeable. Energy can become matter, and matter can become energy. ("E equals mc squared.")

When it is acted upon by energy, matter may take the form of subatomic particles, atoms, molecules, elements, compounds, minerals, vegetables or animals. The changes in matter from simple to complex forms appear to be progressive or "evolutionary" when seen from a temporal standpoint, but the fact remains that both simple and complex forms—from quark to man—coexist at the present moment.

Although a brain is not a mind, it would be a mistake to assume that mind and matter are mutually exclusive. Energy needs matter (in the form of neurons) to produce the sensations and reflections of subjectivity. Without matter to activate, nervous impulses would be mere electricity. Without energy to activate it, a nervous system would be only a network of insensate protoplasm. A brain cannot think, but thoughts (at least as we know them) cannot occur outside a brain. Because the brain is always a part of the body, every subject is an object for itself and for other subjects.

The refinement of a subject's perceptions normally varies in direct proportion to the complexity of its nervous system. With its primitive sensory apparatus, a paramecium can respond reflexively to the grossest stimuli, but it is incapable of reflecting upon its own sensations. The central nervous system of a human being, in contrast, enables the subject to receive stimuli, analyze sensations, conceive ideas, decide among alternatives and take the most appropriate action. A complex subject can feel, think and do more than a simple one.

The more complicated something is, the more the possibility exists that something can go wrong with it. Each working part of a system may malfunction, and so the potential for disaster mounts as the number of such parts or the complexity of their interaction increases. (A simple can opener with a handle and blade, for example, breaks down less often than the kind with an electric motor, revolving turret and magnetic lid lifter.)

As the most complex being on Earth, the human being has the greatest potential for disaster. His elaborate nervous system allows him to be hurt in ways that no other animal can be hurt. With the aid of his memory, he can reflect upon his pain and thereby suffer it all over again.

In order to exist, a mind needs a body as surely as a subject needs an object. The brain is the body of the mind. Thought is a function of the brain just as digestion is a function of the stomach.

Basically, there are two schools of thought concerning the nature of reality: materialism and idealism. The materialist believes that the world is physical, while the idealist feels that it is mental. They are both right—and wrong.

The materialist is right to suppose that objects in the external world are composed of matter and, as such, have a being all their own. Similarly, the idealist is correct in assuming that these objects would not exist unless they were apprehended by the mind(s) of a conscious subject(s); otherwise, they would not be objects of perception. Where the materialist and the idealist err is in thinking that mind or matter alone is sufficient to explain the whole scheme of things.

In truth, both mind and matter are essential to an understanding of the world as a whole. The material object is physical. The subject that perceives it is mental and physical, for the subject has a mind that depends upon a material object (a nervous system) for its being.

It would be a mistake for the materialist to adduce the dependence of mind upon matter as evidence that matter is prior in time and thus in rank. Mind and matter are equally important, as mind depends upon matter for its being and matter depends upon mind for its existence. Furthermore, matter did not precede mind in time. Matter did not even exist until it was first perceived by a mind, however primitive that mind might have been. (Without a subject, there can be no object.)

Time, as we have seen, is a subjective concept. Specifically, it is the perception by a subject of multiple moments in a continuous series. The subject experiences the present moment directly, but the present is always passing away. So those moments that have passed away are recalled by the subject's memory as the past, and those that have not yet arrived are anticipated by his imagination as the future.

The subject attempts to measure the passage of moments by computing the rate of change in the relative positions of two or more objects or else by determining the proportion of one part to another in a given object. Time did not begin until it was first experienced by a mind able to perceive it. Beliefs that the Earth existed for a billion years before the appearance of life or four and a half billion years before that of "intelligent" life are held by present-day minds trying to measure retrospectively the number of revolutions that the Earth made around the sun or the extent to which radioactive potassium has changed into argon during those intervals. Such minds endeavor to count backwards to a period when there was no one around to do any counting—and thus when there was no time. What we now call matter did not exist as an object in time until it was first perceived as such by a subject; what it might have been before that time can never really be known but only speculated upon.

The world is not in time. Time is in the world, more specifically, in the mind of a subject that perceives it. It is pointless to ask when the world began, because it did not need to have a beginning in time. Nor is there any reason to wonder where matter and energy came from, for—objectively speaking—everything comes from *them*—Matter and energy *are* the world.

Q. What's it all about?
A. Objectively speaking, it's about the change of energy into matter, of matter into energy and of energy and matter into various forms of each other. Subjectively speaking, it's about the primal effort to satisfy desire.

Desire is the emotion that causes the subject to move toward an object it finds desirable. The negative counterpart of desire is fear, which causes the subject to move away from an object it finds fearful. (Emotions are subjectively experienced forces that cause motion through distance.) Together, desire and fear constitute the interests that a subject has in the world.

You can want only what you do not have. Once you possess an object that you previously desired, you no longer lack that object and can thus desire it no longer.

In the state of nonexistence, Being is Nothing and therefore lacks everything. That is to say, it lacks existence. Consequently, nonexistent Being desires existence and thereby creates the world out of itself, as everything comes from Being.

Existence splits Being into beings, Nothing into things (subjects and objects). Each individual thing is a part that has been separated from the Whole and that seeks to regain what it has lost. Every thing lacks every other thing and, if it is a subject, feels an insatiable desire for what it lacks.

To a greater or lesser extent, every object attracts every other object in the world. Opposites attract because they tend to compensate for each other's deficiencies. Examples include protons and electrons, positive and negative ions, north and south magnetic poles, heat and cold and females and males. Opposites are drawn to one another because each has what the other lacks.

Being itself desires nothing but existence itself, while existent beings desire other existent beings. Subjects are beings conscious of their own needs, and subjects always desire objects.

The more complex the subject, the more numerous are its potential desires. Food might be the only desire of a protozoan, while a human being may want everything from food to wealth to spiritual fulfillment. The greater the emptiness, the stronger will be the desire to fill it.

Each specific desire expresses the desire for existence in general. In the state of nonexistence, Being is unconscious. It becomes aware of itself and its desire only in the state of existence, in which each particular being desires whatever will affirm and enhance its separate existence. Every subject is conscious of its needs and does the best it can to satisfy them by means of work, that is, by the application of a force through a distance. Unless a lack exists, there would be no desire; and without desire, no action would be taken.

That finite, existent beings should feel needy and try to satisfy their desires for what they lack seems only natural. It is more difficult to comprehend why the infinite Being would create the world in the first place. One possible explanation is that Being had an overwhelming urge for self-knowledge that it could satisfy only by making a world in which it could reflect upon itself as in a mirror. Alternately, Being may have had a yen for something with which to fill its infinite emptiness. Yet another explanation might be that existence is all or part of Being's essence and that Being was inwardly determined to create the external world by virtue of its own nature. These or other possible reasons could be used to answer the eternal question, "Why?"

But the question is meaningless. Basically, reasons are the excuses that we make for doing things we want to do or have to do. Being doesn't need a reason for anything. In the state of nonexistence, where there are no subjects or objects, Being is unconscious, unreflective and perforce unreasonable. Not until it enters the state of existence does perception even begin; reason comes later. Besides, Being can do whatever it desires without being accountable to anyone or anything else in the world, for existent Being is the whole world, or universe.

Desire is the prime mover of the world. Every subject is conceived in desire. Every object is potentially an object of desire. Given the primacy of emotion, it is amazing that people exalt reason as much as they do. (How can creatures conceived by passion expect to live their lives according to the dictates of reason?)

Reason is the servant of emotion. Reason calculates the means to an end—but only after emotion has determined that end. Reason figures how we shall do something, while emotion decides what we shall do in the first place. Reason is relative to desire.

Let's take an example. Please imagine that you live and work in Richmond, Virginia and that you're due a week's vacation that you'd like to spend in Miami Beach, Florida. You're afraid of flying, you hate to take the train and it's too far to walk. So you decide to travel by car. It would be unreasonable for you to drive to Miami Beach by way of Niagara Falls—though it's no more unreasonable for you to vacation in one place than in another; you just happen to prefer Miami Beach to Niagara Falls in this instance.

It's not unreasonable to prefer Pepsi-Cola to Coca-Cola. But if you do, then it would be unreasonable for you to deposit your coins in a vending machine labeled "Coke" when the machine standing right next to it is marked "Pepsi" (assuming, of course, that the Pepsi machine is not empty or out of order).

For every pro, there's a con. For every reason that we can think of for doing something, we can usually think of another reason for not doing it. "It's a beautiful day, and I ought to go outside," we might say to ourselves, "but maybe I should stay home and catch up on my housework. Oh well, I can always do my housework tomorrow. No, I should never put off till tomorrow what I can do today. Still, I should go outdoors for the sake of my health. Or should I? After all, I'd have to breathe all that carbon monoxide and sulfur dioxide; and, with the ozone layer diminishing, I might develop skin cancer or go blind from exposure to the sunlight. Then again, I could just as easily get lung cancer from all the radon in my house. Well, lung cancer's better than blindness, so I'll just stay inside." When we have finished debating the issue, we will go out because we want to go out or stay in because we want to stay in—and that's the only reason that we really need.

Just as the rationality of your actions can be judged by the degree to which they satisfy your desires, so can the truth of your perceptions. A true perception is one that enables you to attain the object of your desire and/or to avoid the object of your fear. A false perception prevents you from achieving these goals. Truth succeeds, while falsehood fails. What works for one person might not work for another, and thus truth is different things to different people.

Desire is the soundest criterion for distinguishing between truth and falsehood. Sensory perceptions can be interpreted in more ways than one. Common sense varies with time and location. Authority may be ill informed or downright dishonest. Logic might mislead us. Science is an exercise in trial and error, and we are always liable to embrace one of its errors. But when all is said and done, we are generally sure of what we want. (We may not know reality, but we know what we like!)

"Truth" is that assumption which people find most desirable. They will continue to believe it as long as it leads to the results they desire. When it ceases to do so or when another assumption produces results that are more desirable, it loses its credibility. Whether or not their desires are the correct ones is beside the point, for what they want is what they want regardless.

When someone tells us to "be reasonable," he's really demanding that we accept his opinion and satisfy his desires. Because each of us has his own desires (and thus his own conceptions of the truth), it is very hard for us to be reasonable with each other. People believe what they want to believe, and they can find logical reasons for their beliefs if they have to.

In the state of nonexistence, Truth is Absolute. It is One, unchanging and universal. Truth is what it is. Truth is Being, and Being is All that there is.

When Being enters the state of existence, Absolute Truth shatters into a myriad of relative truths. In the world, the One has become the many. At any moment, each subject can occupy only one point in space from which to see the rest of the world; and, to each subject, its own point of view is the correct one. Every perception is true in relation to the subject that perceives it. You have your truth, and I have mine.

If you and I were to stand facing each other, we would see the world from diametrically opposite positions. Our viewpoints would be equally true even though they would be completely different. Just because you'd be right doesn't mean that I'd be wrong. Each of our positions would be relatively true, but neither one of them would be absolutely true.

Q. Do you swear to tell the whole truth?
A. I can't, because I know only part of it.

Absolute Truth can belong only to an Absolute Being. With our limited powers of perception, we can lay claim to relative truth at most. Even if an Absolute Being could impart Absolute Truth, we would be unable to grasp what is beyond our reach. Infinite Being cannot relate to finite beings—and vice-versa, as there can be nothing relative about the Absolute.

The relativity of truth makes it impossible for us to settle our differences permanently. We cannot make any statement without incurring the risk of contradiction—because every statement is one-sided, being based on the perception of an individual who can see the world from only one viewpoint at a time. And each viewpoint may be correct in itself.

Frequently more than two sides exist to every story. Naturally, there are as many sides as storytellers. That is why every argument is a waste of breath.

For every argument, there is an equal and opposite counterargument. Whatever can be affirmed can also be denied. As illustrated by closing statements of prosecutors and defense attorneys, words can be used to prove or disprove anything.

So can numbers. A statistician can draw any conclusions he likes from data merely by altering the size or randomness of the sample. If he polled three delegates to the Republican National Convention, he may be able to report that "two out of three persons favor capital punishment." Were he to conduct the same survey on death row, he might find that "everyone is opposed to capital punishment." ("There are three kinds of lies: lies, damned lies and statistics.")

A business owner could instruct his accountant to keep two different sets of books—one set for prospective investors and the other for the Internal Revenue Service. Or an entire government might reduce the magnitude of its budget deficit by partially defraying current expenditures with the proceeds from a trust fund designated for paying future Social Security benefits. ("Figures don't lie, but liars figure.") Of course, it's possible that no one is really lying. Everyone may just be telling the truth as he sees it. (Given the radical opacity of man to man, we can never know for sure.)

In reality, there are no "animals" or "women" or "men" or "Tom, Dick and Harry." These are simply the names that we give to objects of our perception in order to identify and (if possible) to control them. By labeling things, we can classify them and then single them out from others in the same class. A name is the "handle" by which we can grasp an object.

Q. Who killed Cock Robin?
A. Harry Sparrow killed Cock Robin with his little bow and arrow on June 3, 1991, in the Enchanted Forest, in order to collect a bounty placed on the hapless thrush by an unscrupulous feather merchant.

Thanks to our language, we know who did what to whom as well as when, where and why it was done. Thanks to mathematics, we also know the exact day of the month on which the act was committed. Whether or not the information referenced above will be put to use by a dutiful game warden, such names and numbers are generally useful to us in the course of our daily lives: They are the symbols that we assign to things for the purpose of identifying and thereby controlling them.

However, we should not allow ourselves to forget that, as our own creations, these verbal and numerical signs are completely arbitrary. Harry Sparrow's mother could have just as easily christened her son Tom or Dick. (For that matter, she could have even named him Cock Robin.) If we so desired, we could call the shaft that pierced Cock Robin's red breast a bow and the weapon from which it was released an arrow. The month of June could be the month of Jane or John or Juniper. And there is no reason that the symbol "4" (or "5" or "6" or "76") could not have been chosen originally to represent the quantity of 2 plus 1. In the world, there are only objects and the subjects that perceive, name and number them.

The subject apprehends a relative truth by dint of selective perception. Unless an object arouses his interest by exciting desire or fear, the subject relegates it to the background of his perceptual field or ignores it altogether.

An interesting object stands out as the figure from the ground of uninteresting objects around it. As he passes the display window of a butcher shop, a hungry beggar notices the meat for sale but not the price per pound at which it is being sold. A driver approaching an intersection tries to see whether the traffic light is red, yellow or green, but he doesn't care (and thus doesn't see) if the signal's housing is yellow, gray or black.

Interesting objects are meaningful to subjects, and desire and fear are the only possible meanings that objects can have for us personally. We feel ourselves attracted by desirable objects and repelled by fearful ones.

As symbols that stand for the world and its parts, words and pictures mean something. Existence, on the other hand, means nothing but itself, for the world stands on its own. That is, existence stands out from the ground of its own Being. (Existence is that which exists, and Being is what it is.)

We know what existence is because we know the objects that we perceive in our capacity as subjects. In contrast, Being is itself imperceptible, and so its nature must remain forever a mystery to us. We must believe that Being is independent of existence or else accept the staggering notion that our tree in the forest (or at least its essence) would cease to be at the moment that conscious beings ceased to perceive it.

By referring to the twofold nature of creation, we can readily answer two questions that are frequently asked by those who challenge the thesis that we create the world by perceiving it. First they wonder how it is possible for so many different subjects to create the same world in which all of them live. Next they want to know why, if we truly possess the power of creation, we did not make a better world than the one that actually exists.

To the first question, we would reply that all of us do not live in exactly the same world. Each of us constitutes a part of the world, and each of us perceives his own part differently. The world itself would be the sum of all subjects' perceptions—except that no one among us is capable of perceiving such a sum. The world exists in parts, not as a whole, and it can be perceived only one (objective) part at a time by one (subjective) part at a time. To a greater or lesser extent, the world that you perceive differs from the world that I perceive.

But while our respective worlds are not identical, they are similar enough. When two or more of us direct our gaze toward the same point in space and time, we usually report seeing the same object (even though we view different aspects of it from our own individual points in space). The numerous and fundamental resemblances that the sensations of one subject bear to those of another could be speciously explained away by citing coincidence or the similar constitutions of the subjects' sensory apparatuses. The challengers of the creation-by-perception thesis, however, deserve a better explanation than that—and they have it in the thesis of Being and existence.

Being is itself a universe of possibilities, each one a potential object—but it takes a subject to realize that potential. Only perception by a live, conscious being can turn a potential object into an actual one. Only a subject can cause its object to exist, that is, to come forth from pure Being into the impure world of existence. But subjects can bring into existence only what Being has already brought into being, and this is why the beings perceived as objects by different subjects are the same, even though the perceptions of those objects vary among subjects.

This also explains why we cannot create a world that would be more to our liking, one filled with pleasure and devoid of pain. We can make actual only what Being has already made possible. Being has infinite possibilities, but those of finite beings are strictly limited by their individual circumstances.

Restricted to one point in space at a time, each being is subject to the other beings around it. Each subject is subject to its own objects, of which it can never acquire all that it desires or avoid all that it fears. In its desire for existence, the subject creates its objects by perceiving them. It can cause them to exist or not to exist but cannot alter their being, which has already been determined by Being itself. (That's life: You can take it or leave it, but you can't change it.) Being begets all beings, while conscious beings beget existence (through their perception of other beings as well as themselves).

The being of Being is no more open to question than the existence of the world. We know that it is but not what it is—beyond its status as the ground and source of existence. Since Being is infinite and undivided, it cannot be perceived by finite beings that are divided from each other and from everything else. In its pure state, Being does not even exist.

As the Infinite, Being is indefinite. It cannot be defined or limited because it is not one thing among other things. It is the One and Only.

As the Absolute, Being is of a nature to which we cannot possibly relate. It may be an ideal essence ... or God ... or energy ... or all of the above. We cannot say for sure at this point.

Nevertheless, it is tempting to identify Being with pure energy on the basis of the information we now possess. Energy is the capacity for change, even as nonexistent Being is pure capacity, while the world is a place of change and corruption. Being may be regarded as the potential of which existence is the realization. Furthermore, energy exists as an object of perception only when it becomes matter or acts upon matter. It is perceived by a subject solely as the effect that it has on matter. The restless activity of energy even suggests the insatiability of desire. As much as energy invites comparisons with Being, though, the precise nature of Being will always be hidden from us.

We can be sure of our perceptions but not of what they may represent. When a drunk sees a pink elephant, the pink elephant actually exists—for the drunk at least. Whether the pink elephant has a being apart from the drunk's perception is highly improbable—but not impossible. If a sane, sober individual sees a broom standing in a corner, then the independent being of the broom is highly probable—but not certain.

Common sense tells us that things that lie outside us cause our perceptions of the world, but common sense can often lead us astray. (For a long time, it was commonly sensible to believe that the Earth occupied the center of the universe and that the sun and other stars revolved around it.) A "fact," after all, is just an opinion of the majority, and while the majority may or may not rule, it cannot determine what is absolutely true or false. Many "facts" of yesterday are known to be fictional today, and many of today's facts may become tomorrow's fiction. Yesterday, today or tomorrow, all that we can ever perceive are our own perceptions, and what lies beyond them is beyond us.

If the independent being of our perceptual objects is a fiction, then it is at least a useful one. The belief in an external world enables us to perpetuate our subjectivity (i.e., to "survive") and is self-validating to that extent. When we see a tractor-trailer speeding toward us, we do well to get out of its way—whether or not the truck is "real."

Other dividends paid by this belief in a world outside us include the satisfaction of desire and the alleviation of fear. Through experience, subjects learn to pursue objects that afford pleasure and to shun those that inflict pain. As theoretically unsound as it may be, the common-sense view of the world offers many practical advantages to those who accept it.

For all practical purposes, it makes no difference whether objects exist independently of our perceptions. Appearance is reality to the one who beholds it. A mask is every bit as real as the face it hides. Even a dream is real to the dreamer. (The vividness of our dreams at least indicates that our perceptions need not be caused directly and immediately by external objects.) And if we see through a glass darkly, that glass is just as real as whatever may lie on the other side of it.

Q. Last night I went to sleep and dreamed that I was a butterfly. Then I awoke. Am I now a butterfly dreaming that I'm a man?

A. From your own standpoint, you are whatever you perceive yourself to be. If you think you're a butterfly, then act like a butterfly. If you think you're a man, then try to act like one. Either way, just watch out for men who might chase you with butterfly nets.

Existence is the perception of an object by a subject. So is knowledge. Knowledge is perception. Knowledge and perception are one. To know the world is to exist in it and to perceive its parts from a given viewpoint.

There are some things that we can never know and that we shall never need to know. Ignorance is not our biggest problem, and knowledge is not a cure-all for the many ills that afflict us. Knowledge, in fact, can create as many problems as it solves.

When prehistoric man discovered how to make fire, he doomed millions of his descendants to be burned alive. If it weren't for the genius that invented the wheel, thousands of people who died in auto accidents might have lived to a ripe old age. By cultivating plants and domesticating animals, the human race provided itself with the food supply it needed to found a permanent, civilized society—and then to overpopulate it. Electricity is useful for lighting your house and powering your appliances, but someone who has just been electrocuted might overlook its virtues. The potential benefits of nuclear energy are unlimited, but so are the threats that it poses as a weapon and as a source of radioactive contamination. Some scientists try to outdo each other in finding new ways to massacre people and to poison the air and water. The computer is able to perform a host of functions with greater speed and accuracy than human beings, but at the same time threatens to put humans out of work, to invade their privacy or to dehumanize them by processing them into manageable bits of data as factors in computer models. "Progress" may be inevitable, and its price continues to rise, leading the pessimist to believe that things are getting progressively worse.

People who know nothing do not cause the gravest man-made problems; instead, problems generally result from the actions of individuals who may know something but think they know everything. The know-it-all imagines that his relative truth is Absolute Truth. Believing that what works for him should work for everyone, he seeks to impose his own viewpoint on the whole world. If he can present his case effectively, he may attract enough supporters to have his personal desires promulgated as customs, policies or laws. By the time that his followers are able to see the error of his ways, it's usually too late for them to undo the harm that he has already done with their help.

The bigger the intellect, the bigger the mistakes it is capable of making. Only know-it-alls like the rocket scientists at NASA could spend 10 years and two billion taxpayers' dollars on a space telescope with a mirror that didn't work right. (The worst that a moron could hope to do is break his $10 shaving mirror and bring seven years' bad luck on himself.) And not everyone has the brains to design a couple of flying deathtraps complete with loose O-rings and flaky insulation.

Not all of the harm done by know-it-alls is accidental. Look at the wizards on Wall Street. With their ingenious derivatives, credit-default swaps, Ponzi schemes and mortgage-backed securities, these Ivy-League-educated investment bankers and insurance-company executives could inflict far more damage on the nation's economy than some financial illiterate who has trouble just trying to balance his own checkbook.

Schools are like factories in which society endeavors to mass-produce its own know-it-alls. Formal education consists of an assembly line (curriculum) on which raw materials (students) are to be processed (educated) by workers (teachers) into finished products (scholars). In keeping with the division of labor, each worker teaches only that subject which constitutes his own academic specialty. Unsuitable materials (flunk-outs and drop-outs) do not make it to the end of the line (don't graduate).

The end product of the educational process (the graduate) is always a failure, for no student's mind is capacious enough to absorb all the details of every subject taught in school. (And it would be pointless for educators to teach what they did not expect their students to learn.) A total failure leaves school with nothing but a diploma and the realization that he did not learn anything of value to himself. At best, one's credentials and literacy will qualify him for a job whose educational requirements are purely nominal. A partial failure, on the other hand, discovers a partial interest in at least one subject and follows the example of teachers by specializing in that particular field of study. If he keeps on learning more and more about less and less, someday that student might know everything about nothing.

Society is willing to tolerate the shortcomings of its educational system for a number of reasons. First, schools double as prisons in which young people are incarcerated for so many hours each day, while their elders are allowed to spend that time doing socially useful work. (Under a certain age, a person is legally permitted to be in just a few places during school hours: in class, alternate schools, the hospital, jail, a mental institution, etc. Only through truancy or malingering can the student get a taste of freedom.)

The most socially useful lesson taught in school is that of obedience. If the student can learn to obey his teachers, then he will be inclined to follow orders given by parents, police, bosses, judges, politicians, bureaucrats, commanding officers and other authorities. The more apt pupils will be able to acquire skills that make possible the continued operation of society. So even if formal education fails the individual, it rewards the group handsomely.

The details of life are numerous and complicated, but the basic principles are comparatively few and simple. Details are indispensable to a technician who desires to do specific things. They are of little or no importance to someone who simply wants to know whether anything is worth doing in the first place. No one needs a doctorate in philosophy to decide whether life is worth living.

In school, the student begins with subjects that are rudimentary in nature. Progress is measured in terms of the ability to master subjects of increasing difficulty. The student advances from the simple to the complex, attending to more and more details as he goes along. This approach to learning is well suited to the manufacture of technicians who can do the jobs that society wants to be done, but it leaves the seeker of wisdom with nothing to show for his effort. ("Much learning does not teach wisdom.")

A smart person can master complex subjects, while a wise person can understand the simple truth. An expert is capable of analyzing a given topic all the way down to its minutest details, but anything reduced to its tiniest components is mere dust and no longer what it was before its analysis began. To acquire wisdom, one must be able to sweep away the dust that has collected in the course of too much data collection and analysis.

The search for facts is futile because it is too productive. New facts lead to the formulation of new theories, and each theory requires additional facts to confirm or refute it. Every new fact, then, forms another link in a chain that can never bind or even end. In contrast, wisdom is the awareness of what you already know and what that knowledge actually means to you.

A seeker of wisdom will abandon the interminable quest for new information. He desires to get back to basics—the real basics: Being and existence. The wisdom-seeker makes an earnest attempt to see things as they really are and not just as the authorities would have him believe.

This book is one such attempt.

Chapter 2: Pain and Pleasure

Pain is what we fear. Pleasure is what we desire.

Pain and pleasure are qualities of our perceptions. Sensations and reflections can be pleasant or unpleasant. Pain and pleasure are thus relative to perception and may vary from one subject to another. ("One man's meat is another man's poison.") The Garden of Eden, for example, would be Paradise for people who like to camp out a lot, but it would be sheer Hell for those of us who hate the great outdoors.

To be sure, the perceptual apparatuses of conscious beings are comparable enough that subjects experience pain and pleasure under similar conditions. Pain usually signals the threat of injury or death to the organism. For instance, hunger warns the individual of possible malnutrition or starvation; sexual frustration, if suffered indefinitely by too many individuals, could lead to the extinction of the species. Pleasure is often caused by stimuli that promote the well-being or life of the subject. Food helps to ensure the individual's survival, while sex is essential for the propagation of whole species.

We suffer physically because our soft bodies are trapped in a hard world. (No matter how tough we are, the world is tougher.) Our bodies resemble machines that have been built to break down. Unlike machines, however, they have nerves attached to their working parts and so we usually feel discomfort when our bodies malfunction, suffer damage or run out of fuel. With their complex interconnections, our thousands of nerves enable us to suffer in millions of ways.

We suffer mentally because our desires and fears will not cease as long as we live. We can never have what we want because we can only want what we don't have. First, we feel a lack. Then we conceive a desire for what we lack, and we work to satisfy our desire. If we fail, then we feel frustrated. If we succeed, we are happy at the precise moment that we attain the object of our desire and perhaps for a short while afterward. But it doesn't take long for us to get used to our possession and to take it for granted. We can't possibly want it anymore—because we already have it.

Fulfilling your ambition could cause you to be disappointed for more reasons than one. You might find that what you wanted so badly is not really worth all the time and energy that you spent in pursuing it. Even if the object you desired lives up to your expectations, you may never be able to dispel the fear of losing it. (And one day, of course, you must lose it.)

The death of one desire gives birth to a new one, and once we have satisfied that new desire, another one will take its place. The more we have, the more

35

we want. If we are to live without the aid of medical life-support systems, then we must keep striving to attain what we desire and to avoid what we fear. We desire pleasure, and we fear pain.

A life without desire and fear would be boring at best, for it would leave us with no impetus to do anything. Desire without fear produces rashness, leading one to pursue one's goals without guarding against the dangers rife in the world. The fearless individual may experience more pain than pleasure if he can even survive long enough to do so. Fear minus desire equals a life of anxiety in which the tortured subject does nothing but flee from the objects he dreads. He needs an affirmative desire to give him a positive reason for living, something other than his fear of pain and death.

The insatiability of our desires suggests that there is something lacking at the core of our being. There is. It is Being itself.

Pure Being is nothing, but it is the source of all beings. Nonexistent Being is infinite and indivisible, but Being in the state of existence is divided into many finite beings, some of which are conscious. These conscious beings, or subjects, want objects, and their desire is as limitless as the Being from which they came. We are subjects, and all the things that we perceive are objects. We grasp at objects in the hope of filling our own emptiness.

Pain and death are the natural consequences of our finitude and divisibility. Everything that has a beginning must also have an ending—and that includes us. We can be separated into parts, just like any other objects in the world. And in a universe teeming with people and other things, we subjects are always in danger of colliding with objects. Pain, indeed, arises at the borderline between subject and object.

Pleasure is nothing but the alleviation of pain. It must be preceded by a painful sensation. To enjoy food, one must first be hungry. To enjoy sex, one must first be horny. Scratching feels good, but only when you itch. The point is that you have to feel bad before you can feel good.

Pain, then, is the precondition of pleasure. The latter owes its very existence to the former. There can always be pain without pleasure, but there can never be pleasure without pain. Pain is inseparable from life itself.

Life is full of problems, and not all of them can be solved in our lifetime. Unsolved problems cause us pain. Desires and fears that cannot be stilled have a habit of gnawing away at us. If we care about anything, then we have to worry about it; nonchalance is mere posturing.

If you have a body, you have problems, lots of them. You have to fill it when it's empty, empty it when it's full and scratch it when it itches. You must sleep when it grows weary. You must wash it, cut its hair, trim its nails, brush its teeth and blow its nose. You must medicate it when it gets sick and heal it when it is cut or broken. You have to feed, clothe and shelter it and do whatever is required to obtain the basic necessities for it. In one way or another, most of what you do is an attempt to solve the problems posed by your own body. And these problems last a lifetime.

Mother Nature seduces us by making those things conducive to our survival seem pleasant. ("Sugar's sweet.") At the same time, she gives unpleasant qualities to sensations produced by objects that threaten to harm or destroy us. ("Once bitten, twice shy.") We are so busy seeking pleasure and avoiding pain that we seldom have the opportunity to consider whether or not life is worth living in the first place: We reflexively avoid the pain of dying. Pain is a death threat that we find hard to ignore—if it doesn't go away, then *we* will.

The delicacy of our bodies and minds makes us an easy prey to pain. Illnesses, injuries, disabilities, accidents, crimes, wars and natural disasters are among our ever-present possibilities. We are usually unprepared for these catastrophes because we like to assume that such things happen only to other people. It may be comforting to hear that you have just a one-in-five-thousand chance of getting struck by lightning—but not if you're the one who gets struck.

Each living thing is capable of suffering in countless ways. It doesn't take a major disaster to hurt us. A word ... a gesture ... even a glance could be enough to wound the strongest heart. With approximately seven billion people and God knows how many other animals alive today, the sum total of misery on this planet is incalculable.

Although pain or the threat of it is our constant companion, pleasure affords us a temporary escape. Pleasure allows us to withdraw from what we suffer, at least for the moment. To escape from pain is to lose consciousness of it.

We spend half of our time trying to preserve our lives and the other half trying to escape from them. Most of us have to put in at least eight hours a day doing what we would rather not do just so that we can survive. For the second half of the day, we do the best we can to forget the first half. So unpleasant is gainful employment to many people that they find themselves wishing five sevenths of their lives away, yearning for Friday afternoon as soon as they wake up on Monday morning. They have no fonder ambition than to retire.

Escape routes may be natural or man-made. We ourselves may lose ourselves in the contemplation of nature or in a good night's sleep. We might read a book, see a play, attend a concert, tour a museum, take a vacation, listen to the radio, watch television, go to the movies, play games, follow or take up sports, join a club, go to church, gamble, smoke, drink or take drugs. (After all, if nicotine, alcohol and cocaine don't ruin our bodies, then disease, injury or the aging process will.) We may choose a more indirect means of gratification, but the result would be the same. Anything that eases the pain of living will do.

As we have seen, the gratification of the body plays a major role in survival. In fact, many people make it their life's goal to perform their physiological functions in the greatest possible comfort. (The so-called lower animals share this goal.) Pleasure, however, can be mental as well as well as physical.

Puritans condemn pleasure because they identify it too narrowly with sensual indulgence; whereas, in fact, pleasure can take many other forms. A sense of accomplishment, an appreciation of art or the knowledge that one has helped those in need can likewise produce an agreeable sensation. Pleasure is anything that makes us feel good.

We laugh for the same reason that we cry, because we perceive a contradiction between what actually exists and what, we feel, ought to exist. When this perceived contradiction gives us pleasure, we tend to laugh. When it gives us unbearable pain, we cry.

We may be amused, for example, when we see another person trip and fall, because we feel that his action violates his intention as well as the proper standard of ambulation. Besides, we are not the ones who must endure the pain, embarrassment or possible injury. On the other hand, taking the fall ourselves could move us to tears. (It is usually easier for us to bear misfortune when that misfortune is not our own.)

Our relative insensitivity to the plight of others stems not so much from a moral flaw as it does from a perceptual limitation. Put simply, we can only feel our own feelings. Pain and pleasure serve to distinguish the subject from the object. The subject alone feels pleasure and pain, while his objects are what he assumes to cause those feelings.

To each subject, every other subject can be no more than an object. Your perceptions of yourself and the world around you are strictly your own. You can feel for somebody else, but you can never feel with him. You may sympathize as much as you like, but you can never feel his pleasure or his pain. It is a mere coincidence that two or more individuals can be happy at the same time.

A happy life is not devoid of pain. Happiness is pleasure in the long run, and there can be no pleasure without pain; consequently, a happy person is one whose life is filled with more pleasure than pain. Since pleasure and pain are totally subjective, they do not lend themselves to objective measurement, but each person knows whether he is happy or unhappy. The higher the proportion of pleasure to pain in his life, the happier he will be; the lower the proportion, the more miserable.

This pleasure/pain ratio can serve as a standard of personal success, whether you regard life as just a game or as a serious business. If there's more pleasure than pain in your life, you're a winner who's turning a profit. You break even when your pleasure and pain balance each other out. But when the pain outweighs the pleasure, you're a loser who's operating in the red.

Win, lose or draw, we cannot escape the inevitable. Even if life is a game, we must pay to play it. If it's a business, then we have expenses to defray.

Uppermost in our minds should be a determination to get what we pay for. We can always give up the pleasures of life, but we can never give up the pains. Pain and life go hand and hand, and so we owe it to ourselves to enjoy life as much as possible without deliberately causing grief to others. It is our duty to be happy.

In the chapters that follow, we shall examine ways in which we might try to do our duty.

Chapter 3: Hate and Love

Hate and love are passionate interests that subjects take in objects. The opposite of hate is not love; it is indifference, or a total lack of interest.

We hate what we fear, and we fear pain. Pain, then, is the ultimate cause of hate.

We love what we desire, and we desire pleasure. Pleasure, then, is the ultimate cause of love.

Pain and pleasure are the ultimate causes of all emotions. They produce fear and desire, which in turn give rise to all other emotions. Emotions, as their name implies, move us to action: We are moved toward the objects we desire and away from those we fear.

Basically, all emotions are various forms of desire. We fear something because we desire to avoid it. Fear, then, is not the opposite of desire. Fear is the obverse, or flip side, of desire; and it can express itself as panic, horror, worry, anxiety, dread, etc. We feel anger when our desires are thwarted. We envy or feel jealous of someone who, we think, possesses what we desire. Sadness or disappointment ensues from our failure to attain what we desire or to avoid what we fear. We usually desire what we love.

Unless one loves oneself, one is incapable of loving another. The self perceives only its own perceptions, and so it cannot possibly feel for others what it cannot feel for itself. Yet self-love, if carried to extremes, can actually preclude the love of others, as the self may be willing to sacrifice the interests of others in favor of its own. One might go so far as to deceive, cheat, rob, assault or even kill the other for the sake of oneself.

The love of others can produce consequences that are equally horrendous. A lover might make great sacrifices for his beloved—at the cost of much pain to himself. When you love someone, you want to do everything for what you think is his own good; but unless he has actually asked for your help, you run the risk of interfering with his life or of acting in a manner contrary to his wishes. Unrequited love is as agonizing as it is one-sided. Too often, love becomes a desire for the possession and control of the beloved. If you have a rival for the affections of your loved one, you may become jealous; jealousy begets resentment, and resentment can lead to revenge.

Sexual love involves a transfer of energy and matter between two or more individuals, each of whom has her or his own problems. Sex frequently results in the creation of a new individual—with a whole new set of problems. (One plus one, after gestation, can equal three or more.) Too much love can produce too many people, or at least more than the planet can support.

Sexual love is an attempt at "inter-subjectivity." Two subjects ("lovers") try to squeeze into the same space at the same time and feel the same pleasure. They always fail.

Q. Was it as good for you as it was for me?
A. We'll never know.

Those who love things do not expose themselves to the same dangers as those who love people. Thing-lovers never have to worry that their worship of inanimate objects will be repaid with ingratitude, perfidy or contempt. However, material possessions do have the power to own their owners. They can forge an inseverable bond between themselves and their owners by inflaming the latter's obsession with possession. And this obsession, of course, requires money to feed it.

The love of money may not be the root of all evil, as we are told, but a lot of bad things can stem from it. Originally designed as a means to facilitate the exchange of goods and services among members of a society, money has succeeded in complicating things even further. It turns human relationships into financial transactions in which many participants get shortchanged. The failures give more than they take, while the successes take more than they give. Money divides people into classes of haves and have-nots, putting the latter at a social and political disadvantage as well as an economic one. Whether these disparities result from individual merit or from an unfair system, the have-nots tend to regard their condition as unjust. When they do, they are ready to respond with injustice of their own in the form of crime, rebellion or war. When everybody loves money but not everyone can get it, someone is bound to be hurt.

The allure of power is hard to exaggerate. Because we are so small and the world is so large, we need to exercise some measure of control over our environment just to survive. Our environment consists of live beings as well as inanimate objects, and so we are always tempted to treat subjects as if they were merely objects, that is, as if they were instruments to be employed for no other purpose than the gratification of our will. Many people succumb to this temptation, often with disastrous consequences to others and to themselves. ("Power corrupts, and absolute power corrupts absolutely.")

Still, the temptation persists. The more power we have, the more desires we can satisfy and the more fears we can allay, the more pleasures we can enjoy and the more pains we can avoid. Since we love pleasure and fear pain, it is easy to see why we fall in love with power so readily.

Far more difficult to understand is the love of love. Unable to love himself, a subject tries to win the love of others. The subject attempts, in effect, to turn himself into an object of love for other subjects. He seeks popularity, fame or glory in the hope of boosting his self-esteem. Even if he manages to win other people's love, he alienates himself from his own being by subordinating his subjectivity to that of others. The afflicted subject can love himself only if other subjects love him first. The self-image of a subject who is in love with love depends upon the perceptions that others have of him.

In contrast to other kinds of love, the love of knowledge would appear to be a pure and disinterested one. The true lover of knowledge, or "philosopher," fixes his interest upon no object in particular but on the comprehension of the world in general, with the hope of finding the key to happiness for all conscious beings.

Most people who desire knowledge, however, confine themselves to the study of one object or group of objects that represents their own specialty. They may know almost everything there is to know in their chosen field but little or nothing about anything else. Working in isolation, these specialists might learn things that, when combined with other factors of which they are unaware, could add to the sum total of misery in the world.

Eli Whitney, for example, knew a lot more about mechanics than he did about economics or politics. So he probably did not foresee that his invention of the cotton gin in 1793 would help lead to the perpetuation of slavery and to the outbreak of the Civil War—or that even more people would be killed and wounded in that conflict due to the improvement in weapons manufacturing that he made possible with his development of interchangeable parts. A little knowledge is a dangerous thing, as the saying goes, and a little is all that most people can hope to acquire.

Among the noblest kinds of love is patriotism.. Whether his country is right or wrong, a real patriot is ready to die—and to kill—for it. He loves his own country as much as he hates any other country that happens to come into conflict with it. Because so many patriots in different countries are willing to make the supreme sacrifice—or to let others do it for them—it is no wonder that wars are so numerous and costly.

Love, the force that binds individuals together in the same group, also works to drive different groups apart. To form a group, people must feel that they share certain natural or acquired characteristics, such as heredity, culture, nationality, ethnicity, vocation, hobby, political persuasion, religious belief, etc. Those lacking such traits are seen as outsiders, and those belonging to rival groups are looked upon as enemies.

Prejudice results from a group's need for a common enemy. The members of a group may be able to love each other only as long as they can hate the members of another group whose interests are seen as antagonistic to their own. ("It's us against them.") Desiring to foster solidarity among his followers, a group leader may go so far as to create a common enemy if none exists already.

The love of God is the holiest love of all. It is also one of the bloodiest, as exemplified in the Middle East. In this region of the world, Christians fight Muslims, Muslims fight Jews, Sunni Muslims fight Shiite Muslims, and Shiite Muslims fight Druze Muslims as well as other Shiite Muslims—and the members of each sect believe that God is on their side. (Please note that Muslims, Jews and Christians all worship the same God.)

The Middle East is not the only example of how the love of God can kindle the hatred of man. World history abounds with cases of religious bloodshed: holy wars, crusades, inquisitions, pogroms and massacres. When some people believe that theirs is the one true faith, they have no reason to tolerate anyone else's belief.

Some of the worst atrocities imaginable have been committed in the name of love. Contrary to conventional wisdom, love is not the answer, for it turns too easily into its mirror image of hate. What this world would appear to need is less love and more indifference.

Chapter 4: Evil and Good

The optimist imagines that the world is good. The pessimist thinks it is evil. The realist knows that it's indifferent.

The world is not kind or cruel: It just doesn't give a damn. It doesn't care what you or I want, and it doesn't have to. It has everything, it is everything and so it can afford to be indifferent.

You and I cannot. As two more things in the world, you and I lack everything else and need some of those things just to go on living. We desire other things because we believe (correctly or incorrectly) that they will give us pleasure and/or life. Still other things we fear, because we believe (correctly or incorrectly) that they will bring us pain and/or death.

If someone fell to his doom from the top of a skyscraper, the pessimist would cite the incident as an example of the world's evil. The optimist would call it a good thing (or at least a "necessary evil") since, without gravity, all of us would float into outer space. The realist would see it more objectively as the natural result of impersonal forces. (Unless the victim was suicidal, he did nothing to deliberately cause his own death; and even if there were something that he might have done to avoid the accident, such a precaution obviously never occurred to him in time.)

The things of the world are inherently worthless. Value is in the eye of the subject who sees those things as objects of desire or fear. If an object gives him pleasure, then the individual loves it and deems it good. If it gives him pain, the person fears it and regards it as evil. ("There is nothing either good or bad but thinking makes it so.") Death is ordinarily viewed as the greatest evil of all, since it deprives us of everything we love.

Much has been written on the subject of morality—too much. The development of morals is so complicated that we tend to lose sight of their comparatively simple origin. A perception (pleasure or pain) engenders an emotion (desire or fear), which in turn gives rise to a concept (the value of good or evil). It's as simple as that. The matter becomes complicated because pleasure is inseparable from pain.

No one wants evil. Even a "necessary" evil is tolerated only for the sake of attaining something good or of avoiding a greater evil. Everybody does what he thinks best at the time.

Pleasure is good. It is the only good, though it may be either mental or physical. If something feels good, then it can't be bad—at least not in the short run. (And in the long run, we're all dead anyway.)

Pain is always evil. Everybody hates it—even the masochist. (Bear in mind that what "normal" people perceive as pain, the masochist perceives as pleasure.)

Pain could actually be good for us if it served only to alert us to the threat of injury or death. Unfortunately, it does more than this. The pain may persist long after its warning signal has been received and heeded. (Just ask the victim of a fatal but lingering disease.)

Because there is no pleasure without pain, there can be no good without evil. (Sad to say, there can always be evil without good.) Good depends upon evil for its very existence.

Evil is prior to good. Something evil must exist before something good can oppose it. An "evil person" is one who does evil. A "good person" is one who combats evil. Good needs evil in order to validate itself, while evil can stand on its own.

Many people feel that they desire something because it is good, when in fact it is good only because they desire it ... because it gives them pleasure. In the same way, they believe that they fear something because it is evil, never realizing that it is evil simply because they fear it ... because it gives them pain. The value of an object is created by the interest that a subject takes in it. Desire and love engender good, while fear and hate give rise to evil.

People do not always desire, love, fear or hate the same things at the same time. Accordingly, their personal values may differ from each other. One person's good may be another person's evil.

Every conscious being seeks what is good in its own eyes. As far as it is able, it acts in its own best interest. And if this basic endeavor of each living thing seems selfish, one should recall that the self is the only thing that one can know directly. The existence of everything else is inferred from the experience of the self. As the locus of perception, each self is the center of its own universe. It is no wonder that most people are egoists, or self-seekers.

A small minority of individuals are altruists, people who get pleasure from giving pleasure to (or relieving the pain of) other people. Altruists can always find plenty of opportunities to occupy them in this world. It would seem that you can't do enough for other people. No matter how much you do for them, they always need more. ("If we were put here to serve others, then what were those others put here for?")

Also in the minority—fortunately—is the sadist. This curious person derives pleasure from inflicting pain on others. He feels good whenever he can make someone else feel bad. The sadist loves power and needs it to guard himself against retaliation by his victims or their allies or survivors.

Seldom does any one of these three personality types appear unalloyed in a single individual. Each person is usually a mixture of egoist, altruist and sadist. Even the most self-centered egoist will do nice things for other people—as long as he feels that those people will be able to repay him. The sadist will also do favors for others in the hope of enlisting accomplices and thereby augmenting his power. Like the sadist, the egoist frequently injures his fellow human beings—not because he enjoys hurting people as the sadist does, but for the simple reason that he doesn't care who gets hurt as he strives to aggrandize himself. In his single-minded pursuit of what he feels is best for others, the altruist may do more damage than the sadist and the egoist combined. The Holy Inquisitors of the Middle Ages, for instance, tortured people to death in an effort to save their immortal souls. More recently, "freedom fighters" have all but destroyed whole nations in order to make them safe for democracy. ("Better dead than Red.")

The egoist seeks his own good. The sadist feels that what is best for him is to give the worst to others. The altruist takes personal satisfaction in serving his fellow creatures. In the end, everyone is an egoist.

Morals are the values adopted by an individual or a society. If left on his own, the individual would invent a personal code of morality, since each person has his own interests and thus his own ideas of good and evil. To minimize interpersonal conflict, the ruling class of every society imposes its own moral code upon the rest of its members, who are required to view as good whatever their rulers say is "right"; as evil, whatever the rulers say is "wrong."

Morality is applicable only to human behavior. A moralist may regard the actions of nature as being good or evil, depending on their effects, but he would hesitate to label them right or wrong. They just happen. In this view, human nature may be moral or immoral, while inhuman nature is strictly amoral.

To be effective, a moral system must ensure accountability. People can force each other to obey man-made laws, while nature recognizes no laws but its own. Human beings may suffer various penalties for violating customs, mores and statutes, but nature answers to no one. When a typhoon strikes, its victims cannot sue nature for damages.

The moralist needs someone to blame when things go wrong. It is impossible to penalize nature as a whole, and it would be fatuous to punish the "lower" animals for heeding the call of nature. And so, by default, human beings become the targets of his righteous indignation. Humans can be hurt and can be called to account for what they do; therefore, they make ideal scapegoats.

A dog may like to sleep on the sofa because this piece of furniture is more comfortable than the floor. Sleeping on the sofa is good because it gives the animal pleasure; sleeping on the floor is bad because it gives pain (or, at least, relative discomfort). Its master thinks this arrangement is bad because it pains him to see the damage done to the upholstery by the dog, which drools in its sleep. Being the "top dog" in his own house, the master has the power to dictate what is right and wrong to his pet. He either smacks the dog with a newspaper or scolds the canine severely after the latter has committed the offense. Weighing the pleasure against the pain, the dog learns that, under the constraints imposed by its owner, it is bad to sleep on the sofa and good (or at least better) to sleep on the floor.

Unless the owner deludes himself, he does not imagine that his dog has suddenly acquired scruples. He realizes that the animal has merely chosen the lesser pain of sleeping on the floor over the greater one of a whipping or a tongue-lashing. Many people, though, are ingenuous enough to believe that rules and regulations are something more than the orders that masters give to their pets, slaves and other subjects. These orders represent the desires of the masters, which the subjects are expected to satisfy. ("Thou shalt do what I want!")

Just as animals are trained to sit up, roll over and keep off sofas, human beings are conditioned to obey the dictates of their society. The rulers reward their subjects for conduct the rulers love or desire by granting approval, privileges and similar pleasures. For behavior that they hate or fear, the rulers inflict the pains of disapproval, harassment, fines, imprisonment or execution.

Employing rewards and punishments to enforce a moral code is appropriate in at least one sense. The concepts of good and evil originate from the feelings of pleasure and pain respectively, and these concepts are reinforced by additional perceptions of the same kind: The subject learns that he will feel good if he does good things and feel bad if he does bad things. To return good for good and evil for evil is the chief goal of the moralist. Rewarding virtue and punishing vice is what the moralist calls "justice."

The ruling class devises the moral code of every society. Heeding its own conceptions of good and evil, the rulers decide what is right and wrong for everyone else. They and they alone make the rules that the rest of us must obey.

Q. What's the difference between right and wrong?
A. "Right" is what our rulers command. "Wrong" is what they forbid.

Our rulers hold us responsible for obeying them. They make the rules, and we must respond by obeying those rules (if we don't want them to respond to our disobedience by punishing us). As long as we do what they tell us, we can be sure of doing what is good for *them*. We can only hope that they will do what is good for *us* by rewarding our virtue and by punishing the vice of others.

With our help, our rulers may succeed in satisfying their own desires, but they seldom manage to please the rest of us. Everywhere we look, there would seem to be too much evil and not enough good in the world. Even if we ourselves do not feel any pain, we find it hard to ignore the plight of those who do.

It may be the duty of each person to help those in need. Unfortunately, the effort will be at best a stopgap and never a cure-all. There's just too much misery out there.

The individual who attempts to relieve the world of its suffering might as well try to irrigate the Sahara Desert with a water pistol. It can't be done. The most that one could ever hope to accomplish is to moisten a few grains of sand.

But which grains? A true humanitarian would hate to give help to some people while denying it to others. Our sense of justice rebels at the thought of playing favorites.

Like it or not, there are too many people and not enough resources to go around. The resources of the world do not suffice to meet the needs of all who live in it. Despite the best efforts of well-meaning individuals, someone will be left out.

Frequently, the do-gooder does more harm than good. He may have the worthiest intentions, but then the road to Hell is paved with good intentions. That is one reason why there are no real heroes or villains in this world—only culprits and victims who constantly switch roles.

If you're not a culprit, then you have to be a victim, and vice-versa. Often you are both. You just can't help hurting others—or being hurt by them.

Every blessing brings a curse in its wake. For each benefit received, a price must be paid. In the end, every human action is either vain or harmful. It does no lasting good or else it does actual harm.

The individual does not have far to look for the cause of suffering. It's as close as his own body.

All pain is physical, even though we may call some of it mental. The mind, after all, is a function of the brain and the brain is a part of the body. The body is the source of all pain and thus of all evil.

Everyone and everything with a body feels pain. Some bodies suffer more pain than others, depending on their internal impulses and external circumstances. Life seems good to the subject who feels more pleasure than pain. But to one who feels more pain than pleasure, the very essence of existence is evil.

Chapter 5: Necessity and Freedom

Law—any law— prohibits freedom. Whether it has been passed by human legislators or by nature, a law proclaims what is necessary. And whatever is necessary is not free.

The laws of human society prescribe how things ought to be, at least according to those members of the ruling class who enact them. The rulers make the rules by which their subjects are required to live to the letter. Those who make the laws can usually break the laws (or at least have them changed), but the rest of us are not so lucky. ("If the President does it, that means it's not illegal.")

The laws of nature describe how things actually are, at least as far as we know. They represent the attempts by scientists to discern patterns in the otherwise random events and phenomena of the world we live in, and they are continually amended as new knowledge comes to light.

These natural laws apply to everybody. Even the most hardened criminals must obey the laws of nature. After they're born, they must eat, drink, urinate, defecate and die like everyone else. What is physically possible may not always be normal, but it is never unnatural.

It all boils down to the body. As much as we like to talk of soul and spirit, we remain—on this Earth, at least—creatures of flesh and blood.

Everything we do, we do with our bodies. We act, feel and think with them. (Even our minds are functions of our bodies.) Objectively speaking, we *are* our bodies.

Like all other physical objects in the world, we are subject to the laws of nature. Just as electricity produces lightning and hunger impels animals to eat one another, the natural forces affecting man cause him to act in an obligatory fashion. A fly has to fly, an anteater has to eat ants and a human being has to be human.

Essence, or being, precedes existence. Our actions follow from our nature. What we are determines what we do. Being is what it is, and each being is what it is—and therefore does what it has to do.

Nature is the physical essence of existence. It is the way in which objects must interact in the world. Viewed in this way, nature is neither a benevolent mother nor a sadistic shrew. It simply does what it has to do, without charity or malice.

A law of nature is basically a rule of cause and effect, at least as perceived by a systematic observer. In repeated observations, a particular object or event is seen to follow another specific object or event under similar circumstances. Drop an object from any height on Earth and it will fall at a velocity of 32.16 feet per second in a vacuum; it cannot do otherwise. Store water at a temperature of 0 degrees Centigrade and it will freeze; it has no other choice. Stick a piece of litmus paper (or your hand) into a container of sulfuric acid and it will turn red; it could not turn blue even if it wanted to.

The notion of cause and effect cannot be proved or disproved. Although we can never establish that one phenomenon must follow from another, we need to assume as much in order to predict or control the behavior of matter and energy—as well as our own. That many people have died in the past after being shocked with over two thousand volts of electricity does not necessarily mean that other people will die in the present or the future under similar conditions, but it is probably safer to make that assumption than not to. Those of us who are intent upon survival would be wise to avoid lightning bolts and electric chairs whenever we can.

Our bodies place us under the jurisdiction of both nature and society. In the same manner as other animals, we struggle to preserve ourselves by seeking pleasure and avoiding pain. Our desires and fears are the only motives that we have, but they are the only ones we need. Each person's emotions constitute his character, the individual nature from which all his actions flow. Society plays upon our natural desires and fears in order to assert its authority over us.

Authority is the official right to give people orders. It represents one form of power, which is any control exerted by a subject or object over another subject or object or over itself. A person with authority has control over other people, who in turn recognize his power as legitimate. If they do not, then he may have power but he lacks authority. (The late Romanian President Nicolae Ceausescu may have been correct when he insisted in December 1989 that the members of the National Salvation Front lacked the authority to try him for treason, but he could not deny their power to kill him.) Authority—or at least power—always resides in one class of society.

In any society, there are just two political classes of people: those who make the rules, and those who follow them; the rulers and the ruled; the leaders and the followers. The leader gives orders, and the follower obeys them. The leader acts; the follower reacts. The leader has certain expectations, and the loyal follower believes that he came into this world to live up to his leader's expectations.

Membership in the ruling class may be based on birth, merit, wealth, friendship, seniority, tradition, party affiliation or mere chance. A parent can be the ruler of his family; a teacher of his class; a principal of his school; a boss of his company; a judge of his courtroom; a general of his division; or a president of his country. Whatever form it takes, a society is always a dictatorship of its ruling class, where rulers have the final say. Those not in the government are among the governed. If everyone had authority, then no one would have authority.

Rulers have desires like everyone else. Their desires, however, have the force of law. Their followers must satisfy those desires—or else. The leaders believe firmly in law and order—as long as they can lay down the law and give the order. "Justice" is the interest of the ruling class.

Members of the ruled class also have a stake in supporting the established order. Many of them need to play follow-the-leader; otherwise, they wouldn't know what to do. Others believe that they have a duty to obey their rulers or that they will be rewarded for doing so. But the most cogent reason for submitting to authority is fear.

We obey natural laws because we have to. We obey societal laws because we're afraid not to. Authority is the legal right to push people around, while the fear of pain and death is the prod that our leaders use to push us in any direction they choose. They use our fears to satisfy their desires.

Legislators can pass all the laws they like. Judges can interpret those laws to their heart's content. Chief executives can give orders and speeches till they're blue in the face. But unless these officials can count on someone else to back up their decrees, then they're just wasting their energy.

Police officers and soldiers provide the enforcement needed by the ruling class to satisfy its desires at home and abroad. The ruling class recruits its enforcers from the ruled class. A member of the ruled class becomes an enforcer because he needs a job, feels that it's his duty to serve his country or wants to share power with members of the ruling class. (To its enforcers, the ruling class must delegate enough authority to maintain law and order.)

While police officers may be able to safeguard the lives and property of those in the upper echelons of the ruling class, they cannot do as much for you and me. They don't protect us from criminals. They protect us from law-abiding citizens.

The police can't prevent us from being robbed, assaulted or murdered by the minority of individuals who have the nerve to risk legal retribution, but they can and do deter the majority of people from committing crimes in the first place. (Most people would be willing to break the law if they believed that no one could enforce it. Witness the sudden, temporary rise in the crime rate immediately following a natural disaster.) Police officers create the climate of fear necessary to hold society together.

Government itself rests upon violence or the threat of it. It derives its powers from the forced consent of the governed. In fearing our rulers and their enforcers, we do not have to be as fearful of each other.

The very existence of government shows that we don't trust each other—and there's no reason we should. With most people scrambling to advance their own interests, government is one of our few assurances that we won't get trampled underfoot. Our leaders make the rules and then see to it that we play the game by those rules.

The leader wants to be recognized as an authority in more ways than one. To consolidate his position, he lays claim to knowledge as well as power. He is a self-styled expert in his own domain. The parent professes to know more than his children; the teacher, than his students; the boss, than his employees; the judge, than anyone in his courtroom; the general, than his soldiers; and the president, than his fellow citizens. Whether he really does or not, the leader likes to assert that he knows more than his followers about leadership.

And whether he really does or not, his followers like to believe him. The dominant ideas of every society are those of its dominant class. In a large, complex society, people are too busy to examine all the decrees issued by their leaders. Having faith in authority saves them the time and energy it would take to analyze and verify every official statement. Furthermore, their trust spares them the agony of doubt and indecision. They believe because they want to believe. They need to believe.

They are sheep, and fleeced are what sheep are born to be. If they didn't have someone to lead them, they wouldn't know what to do. They seek a shepherd, preferably a good shepherd; but no matter whom they find, the followers always get the leaders they deserve. Even if they do not actively support their leaders, the followers give their consent to the power structure by not actively opposing it. ("If you're not part of the solution, you're part of the problem.")

Leaders feel they are better than their followers, and the followers usually agree. Among other reasons, the followers follow because they believe leaders lead by virtue of superior merit. The prospect of bettering themselves by joining the ranks of their leaders provides the followers with an added incentive for obedience. If they do as they're told, they might get a promotion. Taking orders faithfully may earn them the right to give orders. The only real class struggle is the one put up by members of the ruled class to join the ruling class.

A revolutionary is just a status seeker who is dissatisfied with the status quo. He seeks a new status for himself and his comrades—at the top of a new social order. In a revolution, as the word implies, society travels in a circle and ends where it began. However, most members of the former ruling class have traded places with a few members of the ruled class. We get some new bosses, and the form (if not the substance) of government may change. But, by and large, revolution results only in role reversal. (Those who condemn the Bolsheviks for plunging Russia into a state of despotism seem to forget that the Czars, the Mongols, the Vikings and the Huns were not exactly civil libertarians either.)

In choosing its government, a society has two alternatives. Numerous variations of each and hybrids of both are possible, but essentially there are only two options, tyranny and anarchy. Most societies prefer tyranny.

Tyranny is the logical choice. When only one member of society gives orders and all the rest take them, everybody knows where he stands. One-person rule considerably simplifies the task of administration and promotes efficiency. ("You can say what you like about Mussolini, but at least he made the trains run on time.") No less an "authority" than Aristotle considered monarchy to be the very best form of government.

Democracy, in his judgment, is the very worst. He had good reason to think so, for, in 399 B.C., the democracy of Athens had imposed a death sentence upon Socrates, the teacher of Aristotle's teacher (Plato). Because Aristotle believed that the majority of people are stupid, he felt that stupidity must hold sway whenever the majority rules. He would not have been surprised to see the Salem witch hunt beginning in 1692. But perhaps the best example of direct democracy in action is a lynch mob.

Defenders of democracy dismiss such criticism as being irrelevant. Pure democracy, they contend, is no longer possible in modern nation-states with their bloated populations. No town hall would be big enough to hold all the citizens who might demand a voice in their government, and so critics of democracy are just beating a dead horse. The only democracy worth talking about, insist the apologists, is the representative type.

In a representative democracy (or so the theory goes), everyone belongs to the ruling class—just as in a direct democracy. But instead of retaining power for personal use, the majority gives its power to a minority of individuals who serve as leaders. In a representative democracy, then, the leaders are not the rulers (except insofar as the leaders can vote for themselves and their fellow leaders). As long as every member of society enjoys equality before the law and can participate in free elections, then no individual has a valid complaint against the leaders—not even if they fine, imprison or execute him, for they are simply exercising the power that he freely gave them. That's the theory, anyway.

As so often happens, theory collides head-on with practice. "Representative democracy" is a contradiction in terms. Each person is a unique individual with his own point of view. No one else can see things in exactly the same way; no one else has all the same desires and fears, at least not in the same proportion; and thus no one else's thinking could represent his own on every issue that might be of concern to society as a whole.

If no person can represent another person, it is inconceivable that any elected official could represent the hundreds, thousands or even millions of people whom he might number among his constituents—yet that is precisely what he was elected to do. (The more voters there are, the less each vote counts.) Even James Madison, one of America's "founding fathers," admitted that a "republic" (or so-called representative government) is not a democracy (or government of the people). A republican government may or may not be for the people, but it cannot be of or by them—there are just too damn many of them!

No matter how egalitarian a society may purport to be, it cannot treat all its members equally. Its leaders are human, after all, and human beings tend to play favorites. The leaders cannot resist granting special privileges to those whose social background, political persuasion or economic status most nearly resembles their own. In a capitalist country, for example, there are rich man's justice and poor man's justice. Under communism, one standard applies to Communist Party members and quite another to non-members. Other societies have their own double standards.

Q. Let's be honest, shall we? Did anyone ever tell you that life would be fair?
A. Yes! Everyone did: parents, teachers, judges and politicians. They said that each of us has an equal chance in life if we just work hard and play by the rules. They lied.

There's no such thing as a free election—somebody has to pay for it. Candidates for public office in capitalist societies pay thousands or even millions of dollars to finance their campaigns and so they must solicit contributions from special-interest groups, business owners and other members of the ruling class who have the biggest stake in the outcome of the election. The ruled class pays too, for its members are doomed to be governed by one candidate or another who has won the political and financial support of the big-money interests. (Write-ins and independents rarely stand a chance.) The voters are free to elect only those candidates handpicked by the elite of their society.

Members of other societies fare no better, if as well. They often find themselves voting for only one candidate, the predetermined choice of the one legal political party (as opposed to the two or more predetermined choices offered under a multiparty arrangement). Whereas voters in a two-party system can choose between Tweedledum and Tweedledee, those in a one-party system can vote only for Tweedledum. (Big difference!)

While pure democracy is no longer feasible, representative democracy has never been feasible and never will be. What our leaders call representative democracy is actually a form of tyranny in disguise. Heeding the advice of political scientists like Machiavelli, most tyrants strive to avoid the appearance of tyranny.

The shrewd tyrant will do everything he can to make his subjects think they are free. He will permit elections whether or not the voters have any real choice—or any choice at all. Without depriving himself, he will actively promote the health, indoctrination and welfare of the public. He will pledge solemnly to protect the life, liberty and happiness of each subject. His subjects can believe what they will, perhaps even say what they want—as long as they do what they're told.

In fact, rulers give no more to their subjects than they feel that they must give. "Civil rights" are just a few holes in the blanket of power that our rulers throw over us, and the rulers can sew up those holes at will. ("The Congress shall have power ... to make all laws which shall be necessary and proper for carrying into execution the foregoing powers [enumerated in Article I, Section 8 of the U.S. Constitution], and all other powers vested by the Government of the United States or in any department or officer thereof.") Government provides only enough public services to keep the public alive, useful and dependent.

Let's take a look at our own history. America's founding fathers comprised a group of wealthy and powerful men who got together behind closed doors in May 1787 to decide among themselves how the rest of us should live from then on. Many of those attending the Constitutional Convention in Philadelphia were slaveholders, people who believed that they had the moral right to possess and exploit other people. This helps to explain why the importation of slaves to America ("the land of the free") would remain legal until 1808. (To his credit, the "liberal" Thomas Jefferson promised that some of his slaves would go free—after he was dead, of course, and could no longer benefit from their free labor.) For the purpose of congressional apportionment, each slave was to be counted as three-fifths of a person while Native Americans, who reached these shores at least 10,000 years before white settlers, counted for nothing. African Americans, Native Americans, women and landless persons did not receive the right to vote. After George Washington's first presidential inauguration in 1789, Congress debated whether or not to address the new Chief Executive as "His Highness." The framers of the Constitution set forth our duties and responsibilities, all the while guarding their own rights and privileges. John Jay, the first Chief Justice of the Supreme Court, summed up their attitude when he avowed, "Those who own the country ought to run it." (Throughout its history, America has fought long and hard to make the world safe for democracy; sadly, it has not always displayed the same zeal in ensuring its own safety.)

But tyranny is still tyranny, even when it poses as democracy. Of course, pure tyranny (except on a small scale) is just as impracticable today as pure democracy—and for the same reasons, namely, the size and complexity of modern society. No single tyrant's span of control is broad enough to encompass the multitude that populates an urban industrial nation.

Pure tyranny usually leads to its own downfall. Being human, the tyrant never gets enough of what he wants. He requires an increasing supply of servants to satisfy his growing demand for goods and services. He obtains it by annexing foreign societies (through marriage, treaty, conquest, etc.) or by fostering an increase in the birth rate of his own society (through encouragement of slaves to breed, tax incentives for parenthood, glorification of family life, etc.). Eventually the population becomes too large for him or a successor to manage on his own, and so the tyrant perforce relinquishes some of his power to others. At this point—in which the ruling class is made up of more than one member— tyranny becomes oligarchy. The only difference for the ruled class is that now they have more than one master to serve.

Most societies are oligarchies, or modified tyrannies, because they have to be. As more and more people come into the world, more and more laws must be passed to keep them in line. The ruler feels that, to maintain public order, he must regulate his subjects' lives in almost every detail—from prohibiting murder to telling them when they can and cannot cross the street. The amount of power needed to accomplish this task is too great for any one person to wield, and so several rulers or branches of government must share the power. No single tyrant, after all, can be everywhere at once.

Tyranny begins at home, in which the matriarch or patriarch of the family rules supreme. As families assemble under the banner of a common ancestor, an individual member is chosen to be (or chooses to be) the head of the resulting clan. Clans may unite into a tribe, of which someone becomes the chief. Those tribes that form nations generally recognize a queen, king, premier or president as their ruler. Those that do not are generally vulnerable to the superior war-making capacity of nation-states; hence, the defeat of African and Native American tribes that were too busy fighting each other to present a united front against their common enemy, the white invader.

An empire is a number of nations under the sway of an emperor. Because this form of tyranny is so difficult to administer, empires usually decline and fall. Empires are too large for the modern world; families, clans and tribes are too small; nations are just the right size.

Almost everywhere we look, the leaders give orders and the followers take them. The leaders have desires and the followers satisfy them. Tyranny works.

The only genuine alternative to tyranny is anarchy. Henry David Thoreau, one of its chief proponents, wrote that the best government is one that "governs not at all." In abolishing our government, we could do away with crooked politicians, graft, influence peddling, election rigging, international war and other ills too numerous to mention. In theory, then, anarchy is the wisest political arrangement that a society could make for itself. In practice, though, it's not.

Anarchy is suitable only for loners, those rugged individualists, like Thoreau, who prefer solitude to society. They don't need laws to govern their relations with other people—for they have no such relations. In an overpopulated world marked by economic interdependence, such individuals are rare indeed.

Most people are leaders or followers. Either they need someone to boss around or they feel the need to be bossed. Leaders need followers as much as followers need leaders. ("Lead, follow or get out of the way!") The leader of the flock is also a member of it. The bellwether is also a sheep.

A practicing anarchist has few places left to go in this crowded world, but then the world itself exists in a state of anarchy. In the international community, the power of each nation-state determines its status in relation to every other nation-state. There is no higher authority to which sovereign nations can appeal.

International organizations serve primarily as sounding boards for the mutual concerns of their members. By promoting collaborative efforts among member nations, these bodies might succeed in making the world a better place in which to live—but they cannot preserve world peace. The League of Nations was not able to prevent the outbreak of World War II any more than the United Nations could keep the Korean Conflict, the Vietnam "police action" or a number of other wars from starting.

> Q. How can you be so ignorant? Don't you know that the Korean Conflict was fought between North Korea and the United Nations?
> A. Yes, those were the official belligerents. But the United States was able to secure a U.N. condemnation of North Korea only because the Soviet Union, another U.N. member, was boycotting the Security Council at the time and was therefore unable to veto the American-sponsored resolution. Even so, the U.S. sent troops to Korea before any other member of the United Nations did, and it maintained, by far, the largest military presence throughout the conflict. Meanwhile, the U.S.S.R. supported Kim Il Sung, the "bad" dictator of North Korea, while we backed Syngman Rhee, the "good" dictator of South Korea. The point is that, instead of making collective decisions as a group, the U.N. must stand by while one of its members takes unilateral action and then tries to persuade other members to follow suit. (Judging from the number of allies it has won for its causes, America was less persuasive in Vietnam than it was in Korea. But it was equally convincing in the first Gulf War when it defended the "good" dictators of Kuwait and Saudi Arabia against the "bad" dictator of Iraq.)

Without the power to enforce it, "international law" is a dead letter. Anyone can safely ignore a law that no one else can back up. That is why the World Court cannot truly render verdicts. It can only make suggestions that the parties in dispute are free to accept or reject.

One country may conclude a treaty with another country, but neither can effectively sue for breach of promise if the other decides to violate their agreement. If nations really took their commitments seriously, no major wars would have been fought since 1928, when the Kellogg-Briand Pact declared war illegal.

International disputes can be resolved solely by force or the threat of it. The country that wins the war is automatically in the right. If Germany had emerged victorious from World War II, then Truman, Churchill and Stalin would have been the ones to stand trial for war crimes.

The world is in disorder because there is no one in it to keep order. No single dictator, alliance or superpower has ever been able to rule the world because its different peoples have always resisted such domination. They hold fast to their national identities, preferring to be ruled by despots of their own land than by "democrats" from foreign cultures.

Beholding the chaotic state of the world, individual societies have all the more reason to avoid anarchy at any cost. This they attempt to do by regulating almost every conceivable human activity. For just about anything you can think of, there's a law on the books: thou shalt not kill; avoid, but don't evade, taxes; walk, don't walk. The list goes on and on because new laws are being passed even as you read this sentence. It's hard to make it through the day without breaking some law (that you might have never even heard of).

Society tries to lull you into a false sense of security. If you simply obey all its rules and regulations, it says, you'll be safe and sound. Obey the law and you won't be fined, imprisoned or executed. Don't speed or drive while intoxicated and you will avoid an accident. Study hard in school and you won't be poor. Have a yearly checkup and you won't get sick. Brush your teeth three times a day and you won't have cavities.

Anyone who feels secure is living in a fool's paradise. Such a person is obviously unaware that anything can happen to him at any moment—without warning, rhyme or reason. While you may be prudent to take precautions against problems before they arise, you still have no guarantees against them—no matter how obedient you are. Life itself is hazardous to your health. The world is not a safe place for children or other living things.

Few could argue persuasively that law is unnecessary. Modern society resembles a huge machine whose members are the working parts. The law serves as a mechanical design, specifying how the parts shall work together. Unless each part is geared to work with the other parts, the machine will lose efficiency. If each part is left free to work against the others, the machine may malfunction or even break down entirely. The parts must fit into the whole. The many must function as one.

For any society that wishes to thrive or even survive, law is indispensable. Call it "necessary." Call it "moral" if you like. But please don't call it "freedom," because it's not. Freedom is a luxury that society cannot afford.

We are in the world whether we like it or not. The world presents us with a given number of options and no more. We can take them or leave them. But if we fail to choose for ourselves, then our choices will be made for us. If we refuse to do anything, then something will be done to us.

We may be able to vote for Candidate A or B, to buy Brand X or Y or to watch Channels 2 through 2000, but they are not free choices. No matter how many alternatives we may have, we are not really free unless we ourselves are at liberty to determine the number and kind of alternatives available to us. We never are.

Our internal impulses limit our choices just as surely as do our external circumstances. Even if we were able to create our own alternatives, we could still choose among them only at the prompting of our desires and fears. Our emotions, it will be recalled, determine the ends we seek while our reason merely decides the means by which we seek them. Emotions provide us with motives, and motives move us to act. Each person's motives constitute his character from which his actions follow. ("A man's character is his destiny.")

In deciding among various courses of action, more than one motive often comes into play, but the strongest motive always wins. I am driving down the highway one summer afternoon when I notice a hitchhiker standing on the shoulder of the road. My first impulse is to give him a lift, since I'd like to spare him from having to walk a long distance in the hot sun; but before my foot can depress the brake pedal, I remember reading newspaper reports about hitchhikers who have committed robbery and even murder. While discounting those possibilities, I think of another one: Hitchhiking may be illegal in this state, and, if it is, then I might be subject to a misdemeanor charge for willfully encouraging the practice. (There are so many laws on the books that I can never hope to keep up with all of them.) Besides, it's been a long day and I'm in no mood to engage in any idle conversation that the hitchhiker might care to strike up once inside the car. This consideration, more than any other, leads me to speed past him, avoiding eye contact and feeling guilty as hell. (Happily, my remorse fades as I look in my rear-view mirror and see him give me the finger.)

You may act differently in such a situation. Your desire to help the less fortunate might outweigh your fear of being bored or worse, in which case you would pick up the hitchhiker.

On the other hand, you might make the same decision that I did—but for a different reason; say, you are already late for an important appointment and don't have time to stop for anyone. I myself might give the hitchhiker a ride under different circumstances, or I might choose to oblige him even under the same circumstances—provided that my impulses were different from what they were on the prior occasion.

The point is that, given precisely the same internal impulses and external circumstances, I would act in precisely the same way every time—and so would you. Our actions vary with our impulses and our circumstances.

"Fate" is the interaction of our internal impulses with our external circumstances. Our circumstances stimulate our impulses, and our impulses respond (in the light of reason, if we have any). Our reason may be able to guide and temper our impulses, but it can never suppress them entirely, for these impulses are the wellsprings of our actions. We perform every act because we want to or because it is the most reasonable way (in our judgment) to attain what we desire or to avoid what we fear. Our circumstances facilitate or hinder our actions to the degree that they provide us with desirable opportunities or fearful problems.

There is a myth, usually taken for gospel, that each person (or at least every "sane" adult) is responsible for his every action because he could have conceivably done otherwise. This doctrine of "free will" presupposes that for humans, as for God, whatever is conceivable is possible. But while a human being's will may or may not be strong, it is never all-powerful.

One person can do just so much and no more. In everything he attempts, he is spurred on by internal impulses and reined in by external circumstances. These impulses are his own and no one else's, but he did not create them any more than he created himself.

In fact, each human being does possess free will, though in a narrower sense than is commonly understood. He is free to will whatever he wants, but what he is able to do may be something else altogether. He can desire what he pleases, but that may be all he can do. Internal impulses notwithstanding, he might be quite powerless to alter external circumstances.

We are the victims or the beneficiaries of our circumstances. Under the circumstances, free will becomes synonymous with wishful thinking. I may be willing to run a four-minute mile, but that doesn't mean I'll ever be able to—no matter how hard I train.

The only way to get whatever you want is to want whatever you get. (The ancient Romans used to call this attitude *amor fati*, or "love of fate.") We can eliminate all our frustration if we willingly accept everything that happens to us. Such a wholehearted submission to destiny, however, requires fortitude bordering on the superhuman: Few mortals are able to renounce all their desires and fears and still go on living.

In the absence of external restraints, we might be free to accept or reject existence. If we do the latter, then we are free from everything—for we thereby reenter the realm of pure Being where nothing can touch us, that is, where there are no more things and there is no more "us." But if we accept existence, over which cause and effect appear to reign, then we are embracing life and everything that goes with it, including the pain, the frustration and the ironclad necessity that governs all worldly affairs.

Whatever happens has to happen. Objects interact according to the laws of nature. The presence of subjects in the world complicates matters but does not change them fundamentally. In their embodiments as physical objects, subjects obey the laws of nature; furthermore, subjects are motivated by their natural impulses, the relative strengths of which determine their actions ineluctably.

Freedom is the opposite of limitation. Nature's laws limit nature itself, while both natural and societal laws limit us. There is no room left for freedom (unless we want to think of it as the play in our chains), and without freedom, there can be no responsibility.

Our leaders try to delegate responsibility while retaining their authority. They tell us that, when everything turns out right, we should thank God and/or country. If things go wrong for us, then we have no one to blame but ourselves (and our rulers will blame us anyway).

Moralists and legalists spend most of their time looking for somebody to take the rap. They try to find a scapegoat and make an example of him, hoping to discourage further challenges to authority by instilling fear in everyone else. Their idea of justice is to find fault and punish it.

There is no such thing as a fair trial. A black robe cannot endow any fallible human being with sufficient wisdom to judge another. Since each person is different, no defendant can ever face a jury of his peers. Not all witnesses are truthful, and not all relevant evidence is admissible. Even if it can be proved beyond a reasonable doubt that the accused actually committed the offense with which he is charged, no one—not even the accused—could ever know all the impulses and circumstances that led him to commit his crime. ("Never judge a brave unless you have walked at least 10 miles in his moccasins.")

Nothing is anyone's fault. Each of us does what he has to do—under his own particular circumstances. To be sure, all of us have done things that, upon reconsideration, we wish that we hadn't done. We err whenever our actions fail to produce the results we desired. But we always do what we think is good at the time. If things turn out bad, it's only because we have no way to foresee all the consequences of our acts. Against our will, we make mistakes and have accidents. That's why we may sometimes be guilty, but we are never really responsible.

Necessity is nothing but chance in retrospect. Looking into the future, we cannot be absolutely sure of what will happen. ("*Que sera, sera.*") Looking into the past, with 20/20 hindsight, we can often see that things could have happened in no other way. The simpler the situation, the easier it is to appreciate the necessity of it. But just because we cannot always understand the many factors involved in a complex situation doesn't mean that the "authorities" can.

And just because the authorities tell us that we're responsible to them doesn't mean that we really are. "Catch-22" works both ways. Our leaders can do anything that we can't stop them from doing, but we can do anything that they can't stop us from doing. There are more of us than there are of them, after all, and they can't check up on us every minute.

We have the right to do anything we can get away with. We can jaywalk, speed, evade income taxes or commit murder when they're not looking. Whether we commit minor or major infractions of the law depends, among other things, on how much we are prepared to risk. To those who are unafraid of death, everything is permitted.

Barring the path to such personal freedom is an individual's conscience. Variously described as an "inner light" or as a "sense of right and wrong," the conscience is simply the assimilation of society's values. In the course of his socialization/education/indoctrination, a subject internalizes the expectations that his rulers have of him. Their desires become his desires, and he is normally conscience-stricken when he does not satisfy them.

A subject may feel guilty, for instance, if he cannot bring himself to kill soldiers of a nation on whom the rulers of his own nation have declared war. In the same way, a member of a primitive tribe of headhunters might feel unworthy if he hasn't decapitated any members of an enemy tribe.

Responsibilities must be assumed, duties must be elected and obligations must be contracted. Only labors can be imposed. If you point a gun at me and order me to paint your house, I will surely obey (as long as I'm within range of you, that is). But the moment you turn your back or fall asleep, I'll stop working—even if I haven't finished applying the first coat. I would probably continue if I had initially offered my services to you and you had agreed to pay me for them. Even then, however, I might be laboring under the pressure of an economic necessity every bit as oppressive as a loaded gun. Perhaps I am the sole support of an invalid mother and I have to repay the debts she has incurred. (I could abandon her, of course, but not without suffering pangs of conscience.) Or maybe I must work to support my own wife and children and to repay my own debts. I could have shouldered these burdens under adverse circumstances or at the behest of irresistible impulses. Even if I have only myself to take care of, the fact remains that I did not create myself.

To be binding, commitments must have been made freely. A big difference exists between "copping out" and "opting out." A person who cops out fails to keep promises that he has made. A person who opts out doesn't make promises in the first place. A responsibility cannot be yours if you never asked for it.

No one asked to be born, and so no one is responsible for his own life. No newborn baby ever signed a "social contract" pledging obedience to his rulers in return for the rights to life, liberty and the pursuit of happiness. (As he grows up, in fact, the child may find that life, liberty and happiness are mutually exclusive.) All of us have been thrust into a world that we never made but which makes or breaks us.

From day 1, we find ourselves under the control of nature and society. We cannot even directly influence our most basic physiological functions such as heartbeat, circulation and respiration. We can terminate them only by extraordinary means which are painful or illegal or both. In effect, nature and society force us to live and, moreover, to live in the manner that they prescribe.

The coercion goes on for a lifetime. After years of compulsory education, most of us are prepared to follow orders unquestioningly. "Do this! Don't do that!" bark our leaders. A "good" citizen does what he's told, just as a "good" child is totally submissive to authority. (At least our rulers know what's good for themselves.)

People are no better than they can be. With the mental and physical resources supplied by nature, they do the best they can to cope with existence. They always fall short of perfection because they never have a chance of reaching it. Whoever—or whatever—created them did not match their strength to their burdens. Each person is no more than what nature and society made him. If the pot is cracked, don't blame the pot; blame the potter or the clay from which the pot was made.

In truth, nobody deserves praise or blame. In this world, there are no heroes or villains—only culprits and victims. A saint is little more than a burned-out sinner. Everyone does what he has to do—under his own particular circumstances.

Everything is done according to law, natural or societal. Societal law represents humanity's attempt to repeal the laws of nature, but human nature refuses to be remade. Try as he might to rise above it, man is still very much a part of nature. A "civilized" person is simply a tame animal (kingdom Animalia, phylum Chordata, subphylum Vertebrata, class Mammalia, order Primates, family Hominidae, genus Homo, species sapiens), one whose instincts have been subdued by society. But if its impulses are strong enough, even the most domesticated animal will revert to its primitive ways under the proper circumstances.

Whether or not man is really higher than the other animals, he is more complicated and therefore more unpredictable. The not-so-noble savage always lurks beneath the thin veneer of civilization. It makes no more sense to condemn one human being for preying upon another than it does to censure a lion for attacking an antelope. They just can't help it. Culprits need victims as surely as leaders need followers. In the end, the law of the jungle takes precedence over every other law. The one who is left is the one who is right.

Without natural law, there would be no world. The planets would no longer revolve around the sun. Electrons would stop orbiting atomic nuclei. Elements would not form compounds, and so life itself would be impossible. The world as we know it would cease to exist. Total freedom would be chaos, while total necessity is order.

On the civic level, total freedom would be anarchy, while total necessity is tyranny. Without human law, society would fall apart. To live together, people need law. Law is a social necessity.

There is no such thing as disorder: There is only an order of which we may not approve. The world is divided into parts, the parts fit together into some sort of whole and the parts relate to each other according to some kind of law. It is not necessary to be free, but we cannot be free from necessity while we exist.

It is a necessity that nature has laws in order to exist as a world. Nature has no freedom to do without them. The laws of nature are the only ones possible for nature.

It is a necessity that human society has laws in order to exist within the world of nature. Society has no freedom to dispense with them. At any given moment, these laws are the best ones that society could make, or else it would have made better ones (since it is in society's own best interest to establish the best social order it can).

We are free to do what we have to do. We are free to be what we have to be. Nothing more.

Chapter 6: Poverty and Wealth

Even if money can't buy happiness, it's better to be unhappy with money than without it. Money can buy the things that we want and need. The lack of it can cause no end of problems, so we tend to assume that more money means fewer problems. We usually associate wealth with pleasure and poverty with pain. For these reasons, most of us desire wealth and fear poverty.

At first glance, money would not seem to have as much value as it does. Those little green bills are pretty enough, but you can find better artwork in a comic book. What's more, you can't eat, drink, drive, wear or inhabit Federal Reserve notes—so what good are they? At least the metal coins can be used to play tiddlywinks, and they cost more to produce than paper money—yet the average coin is worth less than the average dollar bill. How come?

The answer, in part, is that cost does not necessarily equal value. The value of an object lies in its ability to satisfy a desire. An object has use value when it can serve directly as food, clothing, shelter, medicine, etc. If need be, a potential user will incur any affordable cost (that is, make any reasonable sacrifice) to obtain the object of his desire, even if he is the only person who might find a use for it.

Market value, on the other hand, refers to the power of an object to command other objects in exchange. Ideally, the market price of an object is the highest one that a buyer would willingly pay and the lowest one that a seller would willingly charge for it in an open and competitive market. In terms of market value, the worth of a thing is what it will bring, no matter what it cost to make or what it can be used for.

A given object may have use value or market value or both—but only if somebody gives it value by desiring it. (A useful commodity is called a "good" because it can satisfy a desire.) In any case, value is really in the subject, not the object. An item has value only because somebody thinks it does.

Money has value only because our rulers tell us it does and we believe them. The government selects a monetary unit and declares it to be the standard of value and the medium of exchange for everyone in its jurisdiction. In the United States and Canada, the monetary unit is the dollar; in Mexico, it is the peso; in Great Britain, the pound; in France and Germany, the euro; in Russia, the ruble; in China, the yuan and in Japan, the yen—but it could be anything anywhere, depending on the whims of the rulers.

The monetary unit could just as easily be (and actually has been) tobacco, salt, cattle or seashells. In 1685, when the colonial governor of Canada had not received enough official currency from France to pay his troops, he decreed that ordinary playing cards would serve as legal tender so long as each one bore his signature. The troops believed him, and his scheme worked. (It couldn't fail, as long as the subjects accepted their ruler's word as final.)

The only reason that the money issued by the Second Continental Congress and the Confederate States of America proved to be worthless is that the citizens of colonial America and those of the Confederacy did not believe that their respective governments were strong enough to enforce their decrees. Money may be "backed by the full faith and credit" of the government, but it has no value unless the citizens have faith in that government and are willing to give it the credit it needs.

The basing of money on a gold standard does not change the arbitrary nature of its value. Apart from jewelers and dentists, few people can find any practical purpose for gold. (King Midas learned this lesson the hard way.) Like money, gold is short on use value but long on market value, and, like money, it has market value because people think it does. "Money talks" only when people put words in its mouth.

As long as people believe that money is worth something, they will continue to work for it. Their willingness to perform labor in exchange for it constitutes its value. It's not the paper, ink, bronze, copper, nickel, silver or gold that makes money valuable; it's the willingness of people to work in return for it.

Everything on Earth is inherently worthless. An object has value for no other reason than that somebody desires it. It acquires use value only after somebody does work on it. Nature provides the raw materials, but man must furnish the labor to turn them into usable commodities. Food must be gathered, hunted or raised; clothing must be fabricated; houses must be constructed. Not so much as a pebble can be used until someone stoops to pick it up. An object possesses market value when a prospective purchaser is willing and able to spend enough money to make its owner part with it.

Spending money is one way of expending labor. If money is to have value beyond the cost of the materials used to produce it, it must somehow represent the time, energy or skills needed to produce goods and provide services. In a conveniently portable form, money symbolizes labor.

I go to the grocery store and buy a loaf of bread, but my dollar has to pay for more than the actual ingredients of the bread and the plastic in which it is wrapped. It must help to pay for the overhead and equipment of the store and the salaries of its employees. When the store manager buys that same loaf of bread from a wholesaler, he must likewise pay—in part—for the overhead, equipment and salaries at the bakery. The baker must pay, among other suppliers, a farmer to grow and harvest wheat, rye or corn; a refiner to purify sugar from cane or beets; a miner or brine-well operator to extract salt from the Earth and chemical-plant managers to process yeast and shortening. None of these suppliers would sell the baker what he desires unless they were sure that the baker could compensate them with something they could use to buy the things that they desire. Under normal economic conditions, the baker would not sell the bread to the store manager if he did not believe that the latter would be able to reward him sufficiently for producing and distributing it. And the store manager (or his employee) would not sell it to me without some assurance that he will receive enough in return for going to the trouble of buying it wholesale and merchandising it. Whether or not everyone gets what he deserves, one thing is certain: By the time the bread reaches my hands, a lot of people have done a lot of work on it. Nature may have furnished the basic ingredients, but it took a host of skilled human beings to combine those ingredients into something I can eat—and those human beings needed a better reason than my nourishment to perform their various labors.

Money is reason enough. If I can give you something you want, then you may be willing to give me something I want. Since most of us want money, money provides us with a universal incentive to work for each other. Money gives us the assurance we need that the hire is worthy of the laborer.

For five or more days per week, a jobholder gives his employers what they want, namely, his labor. At the end of the week, the employers give him what he wants, namely, money. After paying taxes to the rulers and putting something aside if he can, the jobholder gives what is left of his salary to various business owners and professionals in exchange for the objects of his desire, namely, the goods and services they offer. People do what they may not want to do (work) in order to have what they want to have (money and the things that money can buy).

Money entitles the one who possesses it to command the labor of others. If you have more money than I do, I have to work for you. If I have more money than you do, then you must work for me. The more money a person has, the less work he has to do for other people.

If you have more money than I do (and you probably do), then I might be a clerk in your store or a hand in your factory, but I don't have to be your employee to work for you. I may wait on tables at your favorite restaurant, or I could drive the bus that takes you to work in the morning. Perhaps I teach your children in school—thus cooping them up and keeping them out of your hair for seven hours a day or longer. I may function as a petty bureaucrat in your local government. I might own and manage a company that manufactures a product you buy—or maybe I operate another firm that produces a competing item and thereby helps to keep down the price of the product you favor. One way or another, I work for you as long as I do anything that is even remotely useful to the society in which you live. Everyone makes an economic contribution to society when he provides a good or service that is not illegal.

If I were rich enough, I wouldn't have to work for anyone else. I might choose to spend my whole life serving humanity—but I would be under no economic compulsion to do so. With enough money in the bank, I could stop working for others and work for myself alone—or stop working altogether.

When I am rich enough to work for no one but myself, the line between work and play blurs until it vanishes. Technically, work is the movement of a force through a distance, and so I do work in a physical sense whenever I lift a spoonful of soup to my mouth or walk upstairs to bed each night. I expend even more energy when I play a game of tennis. However, in the more restrictive sense of economics, I work only when my efforts produce a good or service that could be sold on the market: No matter how hard I strain to build a ship in a bottle or to write my personally meaningful diary, I do so to satisfy my own desires and not those of a boss, client or customer. If I strove to amass an even greater personal fortune than the one that already permits me (in my dreams) to live a life of self-indulgence, I'd be acting out of greed rather than financial necessity. Wealth would allow me to please nobody but myself.

Q. How much is enough?
A. There's never enough!

Q. Where do you draw the line between ambition and greed?
A. You can't.

Wealth would also give me the option of not working at all. ("*Dolce fare niente*: It is sweet to do nothing.") I would not even have to work for myself, since I could find enough people who would be willing to work for me. They would do anything (or almost anything) that I paid them to do. In purchasing goods and services, I pay others to do the work that I would otherwise have to do in order to provide myself with the things I want. (For the right price, I could even get someone to build a ship in a bottle or to write my diary for me.)

We tend to envy others for having to do less work than we do—as much as we envy them for having more money than we have, since it often amounts to the same thing. ("If I were a rich man," sang Tevye in *Fiddler on the Roof*, "I wouldn't have to work hard.") Many of us resent able-bodied people on welfare not only because we have to support them with our taxes but also because they violate the first rule of the game that the rest of us play: People are supposed to stop working only after they've made a fortune or earned a pension. (Of course, few of us would care to trade places with welfare recipients. We might enjoy their life of leisure—but only if our standard of living could be a lot higher than theirs.)

Many people desire to be "independently wealthy." They believe that, if they have enough money, they won't have to depend on anyone for what they need. They are mistaken. The richest person in the world must still rely upon others to provide him with the necessities and luxuries of life, unless he can do everything for himself as Robinson Crusoe could. (And even Mr. Crusoe found that Friday was a good man to have around.)

Robinson Crusoe was independent, whereas Andrew Carnegie was wealthy. The latter gentleman depended on other people to do almost everything for him, even to run his steelworks. For his own epitaph, the candid Mr. Carnegie chose the following words: "Here lies one who knew how to get around him men who were cleverer than himself."

To be alive is to be in need. The rich are every bit as needy as the poor—the only difference is that the rich are in a better position to satisfy their needs (with the labor of the poor). You can have wealth or independence or both, but being wealthy doesn't make you independent.

The majority of people would prefer wealth. They would just as soon let someone else bake their bread, make their shoes and patch their roofs. The average person would like to have enough money to be able to stop working, but, after due consideration, he hopes that such good fortune would not be shared by everyone else. He comes to realize that if everyone stopped working, then everyone might as well stop eating too. There would soon be no food or anything else to buy, for no one would produce, distribute or sell anything—because everybody would be too "rich" to bother. In the event of a universal work stoppage, money could no longer be put to its one practical use as a medium of exchange, and everyone would learn that the only real value of money lies in the labor that it is supposed to symbolize.

Many economists would say that labor is just one among several of the components of value. Among the others must be counted land, capital and management. Land, in their view, includes all natural resources. Capital, management and labor constitute the human resources needed to produce something of value. (Of course, humanity is a part of nature, and so the distinction between human and natural resources is made purely for the sake of convenience.)

Land, everything on it and everything in it, is worthless until somebody labors upon it. The land itself must be cut, filled and tilled. Unless they are picked in the wild, fruits and vegetables must be planted, watered, fertilized and harvested. Trees must be cut down and cut up. Rivers need to be dammed. Animals must be bred, fed, milked, fleeced, slaughtered and skinned—or at least hunted. Gold, silver and other minerals have to be mined. Unless it is forced to, the Earth will not yield anything of value to human beings. ("In the sweat of thy face shalt thou eat bread, till thou return unto the ground.")

Capital is defined as wealth used to produce more wealth. Examples of it include tools, equipment, machinery and factories, all of which are produced by human labor. Loosely speaking, money is a form of capital, but only when money is used to finance a business venture or the formation of more capital. (In any case, money has value only when it symbolizes labor or the product of labor.)

Those who dispute the "labor theory of value" come closest to disproving it when they cite management as a factor of production. At first glance, the activities of management (e.g., lounging in an air-conditioned office, reading *The Wall Street Journal*, dictating memos, hiring and firing workers, sipping martinis at a three-hour "power lunch" if the manager is a corporate executive and taking an 8-hour coffee break if he's a government bureaucrat) would seem to have little in common with labor as we know it. Unless they are playing golf, managers seldom move a force through a distance, and so they appear to do no work at all.

Yet, management is vital to the productive process, in which the efforts of numerous individuals must be coordinated and directed to the attainment of a common goal. Someone must decide exactly what is to be done and how it is to be done. The job of a manager is to see that his subordinates do their jobs. He does the mental work of planning, organizing and controlling the physical work done by others, trying to make sure that the task is completed on time and without going over budget. This is the function of management, and it is so important to employers that they are willing to reward their top executives with astronomical salaries and luxurious perquisites in return for performing it. ("It's a dirty job, but somebody's gotta do it!")

Somebody has to crack the whip. Most people don't like to work, and therefore someone has to stand over them every minute to see that they do what is required of them. Slaves need masters just as any other followers need leaders.

Those in the ruling class are the masters, and the rest of us are their slaves. Of course, we don't like to think of ourselves as slaves, and for that reason we refer to our rulers in the workplace as "supervisors" or "bosses" instead of masters, but the distinction is merely semantic. (In fact, supervisor means "overseer" in Latin, while boss derives from the Dutch word for "master.")

It is the lot of a slave to satisfy the desires of his master rather than his own. A slave is a person who is forced to labor for another person. Slavery has always existed in the world, and it always will. The only thing that changes is the form. This peculiar institution probably originated when one tribe vanquished another and decided to exploit the labor that could be furnished by prisoners of war. (Some anthropologists believe that slavery marked a significant advance in civilization, because it was more humane [and more profitable] than the prior custom of putting all conquered foes to death.)

Slavery soon spread throughout the "civilized" world, victimizing war captives, women, Africans, political prisoners, debtors and poor people in general. Bondmen, serfs, apprentices and indentured servants performed the most grueling and unpleasant tasks as they watched their masters live off the proceeds of this forced labor. Today, "wage slaves" do all the dirty work while their bosses earn a lot more for doing a lot less; business owners may not do anything at all. Anyone who has to work for a living is a slave.

Beginning in 18th-century England and spreading to America and Continental Europe, the Industrial Revolution altered the style of slavery but left its substance intact. Chattel slavery had been ideally suited to an agrarian society in which human muscle provided most of the power required to produce the necessities of life. When steam and electricity began to drive the machines recently invented for the cotton and iron industries, however, the locus of production shifted from the country to the city and from the home to the factory. For the purpose of mass production, a new kind of slave was needed.

Whereas slaves had traditionally been purchased for their lifetimes, the new bondmen were rented by the hour. The boss, as a factory owner, had so much money tied up in his plant and equipment that he could not afford to spend any more on labor than was absolutely necessary; thus, he preferred a work force that could be expanded or contracted as demand for his product grew or shrank. He wanted to be able to hire more workers when business was booming and to lay them off when the market softened.

Unlike the slave owner, who needed to protect his sizable investment in labor by guaranteeing at least the subsistence of his slaves or serfs, the factory owner had but to offer a "competitive" wage. A slave owner had to care whether his slaves lived or died; a boss didn't. If wage slaves perished in their economic struggle for existence, they could be replaced cheaply and easily. The factory owner did not even need to go hunting for replacements—they would come to him, looking for work.

They came from the countryside to the cities that had been hastily built around the new factories. At first, wages were high in comparison with what people could earn from farming or from selling goods they made by hand in their homes and shops. But the factory owners began to recruit poverty-stricken immigrants, women and children into the work force. By thus flooding the labor market, the bosses no longer needed to offer decent pay and working conditions. If an employee wanted to quit his job, the factory owner could find many others eager to take it. By that time, it was too late for factory workers to go back to the farm, where inventions like the sowing drill, the reaper and the thresher had reduced the need for their services. The handicraftsmen could not hope to compete with machines either.

Consequently, self-sufficient farmers and independent artisans gave place to hired hands. They were trapped—in squalid tenements and hazardous sweatshops. They suffered hunger, disease and dismemberment, while their bosses rolled in the lap of luxury. The lower the bosses could keep their labor expenses, the greater were the profits they could expect to make.

And the profits were enormous. Enlarging the scale of operations as demand for their products increased, the business owners built so many new factories that they no longer had enough time to run each one personally. Instead, they concentrated on seeking new opportunities to invest their profits. While retaining ultimate authority for making decisions concerning policies and objectives, the owners left the day-to-day operation of their businesses to an emerging class of professional managers.

Factory owners were the masters of wage slaves, and managers became the overseers or slave drivers. The manager oversaw, or supervised, workers to make sure that they lived up to the expectations of the owner. The owner's desires became the manager's desires. And it was the zeal of the manager in promoting his boss's interests as a worker, toady or informant that originally won him a promotion to the ranks of supervision from those of labor. (This recalls the practice of the Southern plantation owner of upgrading his favorite field slaves to the status of house slaves, in which capacity they enjoyed greater privileges than their fellow slaves and came to exercise power over the latter.)

While the Industrial Revolution hastened the demise of traditional slavery in Europe, it paradoxically gave new life to this institution in the United States. Great Britain's burgeoning demand for raw cotton encouraged the antebellum South to perpetuate an economy based solely on agriculture. The South had no incentive to industrialize when its planters could sell to British textile mills as much cotton as their slaves could pick. And the invention of the cotton gin only made matters worse for the slaves and better for their masters. American slave owners did not have to relinquish their human chattels until the end of the War Between the States, when the North forced the South to realize that the only "rights" possessed by the states were those that the stronger national government allowed them to have. (Justice is the interest of the ruling class.)

Emancipation hurt the slave owners more than it helped the slaves. The planter lost his unpaid labor, but the former slave did not gain much in the bargain. In effect, the Thirteenth Amendment to the Constitution created a new class of homeless persons who quickly fell prey to official discrimination (in the form of Jim Crow laws and Southern "black codes"), intimidation and violence. African Americans initially received economic assistance from the Freedmen's Bureau of the U.S. Government, but they lost it when this agency was dissolved in 1872. And they could no longer count on political support from "carpetbaggers" and "scalawags" when, in 1877, President Rutherford B. Hayes withdrew the last federal troops from the South to keep a promise he had made in order to steal the 1876 election from his Democratic opponent, Samuel J. Tilden. (Tilden had received 160,000 more popular votes than Hayes, but the stubborn Republicans claimed victory in the electoral college. To persuade Southern Democrats to surrender the presidency to him, Hayes offered to remove the last vestiges of Reconstruction—and the Democrats accepted. Of course, Hayes never bothered to ask Southern blacks what they wanted, since they did not have political clout.)

Abandoned by their "liberators" and left economically destitute, the former slaves had to beg their former masters for employment. The traditional slavery of whips and chains became the neo-slavery of underpaid labor and tenant-farmer contracts drawn up by the landlord to favor himself.

African Americans met with as much intolerance up North as they did down South—and for the same reason. They were forced to compete with poor whites in the job market. To compound the problem, native-born Americans of all races had to vie for employment with immigrants. The struggle for a livelihood pitted one group of workers against another, lowering wages and heightening ethnic tensions.

Encouraging these rivalries—and profiting handsomely from them—were the railroad barons and captains of industry (as well as the bankers financing their operations) whose fortunes had been growing steadily since the Civil War had created a need for transportation, production and investment on a larger scale than ever before. These bosses of big business played off one group against another—blacks against whites, natives against immigrants, Asians against Europeans, northern Europeans against southern Europeans, western Europeans against eastern Europeans, etc. For their poverty and dismal working conditions, the members of each group blamed a rival group or groups instead of their bosses, who handed out the paychecks after all. (Humans and other animals learn to love the ones who feed them and to hate those who compete with them for food or any other desirable object.)

As the boss weakened the position of his workers by dividing them, he strengthened his own by uniting with other bosses to minimize competition and maximize profits. Businesses began to form monopolistic trusts, cartels and other combinations in restraint of trade. The bosses bristled, however, at the prospect of their workers organizing to bargain collectively with them. To the economic threat posed by labor unions, big business responded with lockouts, court-ordered injunctions, restrictive legislation sponsored by elected officials whose political campaigns they bankrolled and armed force supplied by government troops or professional strikebreakers. The rich built a wall between themselves and the poor, hoping that it would be too high for most poor people to surmount, but not high enough to discourage indigents so completely that they might try to knock it down.

The wall threatened to crumble after the stock market crash of 1929. Farm prices fell. Thousands of banks and businesses failed. Millions of people lost their jobs, homes and life savings. Even some formerly rich people had to push apple carts or stand in bread lines that stretched for blocks. America was ripe for revolution, as agitators exhorted the poor to turn society upside down. The rich needed an advocate of their own.

The spokesmen they already had were doing more harm than good to their public image. Promising that prosperity was "just around the corner," President Herbert Hoover urged Americans to repose total confidence in the ability of business leaders to resolve the economic crisis. While reluctant to grant direct relief to the poor, Hoover was more than willing to give government loans to businessmen and to cut their personal and corporate income taxes, imagining that the extra money in their coffers would somehow "trickle down" to the working classes. His Secretary of the Treasury, multimillionaire Andrew Mellon, saw the Great Depression as a normal consequence of the business cycle with which government should not interfere—no matter how much suffering followed. "Liquidate labor," he advised. "Liquidate stocks. Liquidate the farmers." (Talk like this was more likely to get rich people lynched than reelected.)

To forestall a slave revolt and maintain their status as that of the ruling class, rich people had to find someone who could convince poor people that the rich had the poor's best interests at heart. Rich people needed a champion.

They found two, the husband-and-wife team of Franklin and Eleanor Roosevelt, and no two individuals could have been better suited to the roles they were called upon to play. They came from wealthy families. He was a cousin of President Theodore Roosevelt, and she was Teddy's niece. From an early age, both had grown accustomed to being waited on hand and foot. Neither had to worry about making a living; their careers, in effect, were their hobbies. Both were charismatic crowd-pleasers. While the First Lady toured America, preaching the universal equality of all human beings (a sentiment warmly applauded by the poor), President Roosevelt broadcast his folksy "fireside chats" (during which he addressed his listeners as "my friends" and offered a "New Deal" for the "forgotten man").

FDR vowed to use "the authority of Government as an organized form of self-help for *all classes* [emphasis added] and groups and sections of our country." He wasn't trying to abolish the class structure of American society; he was doing his best to maintain it. Instead of a real revolution, he offered a make-believe one.

In the eyes of ultraconservative bankers, business owners and Supreme Court justices, his program was revolutionary nonetheless. President Roosevelt continued Hoover's policy of promoting industrial recovery, but where his predecessor had given away money with no strings attached, Roosevelt insisted on regulating the businesses he aided—much to the dismay of business owners. (Business owners seem to love government contracts, subsidies, loans, loan guarantees and bailouts—as much as they hate "government interference.")

Direct relief to the poor was part of Roosevelt's program, but he placed the major emphasis on public works. The poor continued to satisfy the desires of others, but now their bosses were government bureaucrats instead of corporate executives. FDR did everything he could, from protecting labor unions to sponsoring wage-and-hour legislation, to make work seem less like slavery. But, in the end, workers were still slaves toiling for masters.

Anyone who mistook President Roosevelt for a bleeding-heart liberal should have taken a closer look at his agricultural policies. At a time when many

Americans didn't have enough to eat, FDR paid farmers to let their fields lie fallow lest they "overproduce" and thereby depress farm prices even further. So committed was he to reducing the agricultural surplus that he ratified a decision made by his Secretary of Agriculture, Henry Wallace, to plow under millions of acres of crops (purchased with federal funds) and to buy and slaughter 5,000,000 pigs—rather than let this food fall into the hands (and mouths) of hungry citizens who couldn't afford to pay for it. "To destroy a standing crop goes against the soundest instincts of human nature," conceded Secretary Wallace, but he hastened to add that "agriculture cannot survive in a capitalistic society as a philanthropic enterprise." (In other words, capitalism and compassion don't mix: Capitalistic society is a rat race that only rats can win.)

For that reason, it took a tougher guy than Franklin Delano Roosevelt to end the Depression. It took an Adolf Hitler.

Few people suffered more during the Depression than the Germans. As if the economic downturn weren't bad enough, they were also required to pay over $31,000,000,000 in reparations for their "total guilt" in having allegedly started the First World War all by themselves. (Even President Woodrow Wilson had thought that the amount of reparations and the war-guilt clause of the 1919 Versailles Treaty were unfair, but he caved in to demands made by England and France.) Afraid that millions of their unemployed countrymen would embrace communism, the wealthy barons and industrialists who comprised Germany's ruling class financed the successful political campaigns of Hitler and his National Socialist Party. Before long, Hitler had repudiated the peace treaty, rearmed Germany and started the Second World War. Germany was off and running again.

England and France, put together, were no match for Germany, and so they had to ask the United States for help. For the ailing U.S. economy, their request could not have come at a better time. The market for armaments at first put pounds and francs (and later, with America's entry into the war, federal dollars) into the pockets of American manufacturers and those they hired. Like its European counterparts, the U.S. Government subsidized the construction, conversion and expansion of factories to meet the rising demand. Formerly jobless persons who were not drafted into the armed forces could find work in defense plants.

It was World War II, not the New Deal, which really put workers back to work and business owners back in business. FDR did everything by halfway measures ... until Hitler made him go whole hog. The federal government coordinated the activities of business, industry and agriculture. It told manufacturers what to produce and farmers what to grow, allocated strategic raw materials, rationed critical goods, controlled prices and wages, froze rents, insured mortgages and even built new houses for defense workers. In consequence, the rich got richer as usual. Even so, the poor never had it so good. (Many of them, in fact, rose to the ranks of the so-called "middle class.") World War II pulled America out of the Depression—albeit at a cost of over 400,000 American lives.

More often than not, war is good for business. When the economy starts to cool down, a war can heat it up again. Goods must be produced and services must be provided to fuel the war effort. If nothing else, war makes the Gross Domestic Product grosser.

To go on enjoying the benefits of World War II without suffering as many casualties, the ruling classes of the United States and the Soviet Union decided to wage a "Cold War" against each other. What they sought was no less than a "war in peace" that would permit American business owners to maximize their profits and Soviet leaders to maintain the "dictatorship of the proletariat" (i.e., the dictatorship of the Communist Party) so that the latter might stave off the threat of "capitalist encirclement." The Cold War was to be less of a war than a war game in which both sides would assume threatening postures toward each other but neither would have to fire a single shot—unless one side dared to break the rules of the game by actually encroaching on the other's territory or sphere of influence. The penalty for such a breach was to be a "limited war," a type of conflict with rules of its own.

In limited wars, the U.S. and the U.S.S.R. fought each other by proxy. One side backed the ruler of an unstable nation (usually a dictator), while the other supported a rebel faction or a foreign ruler (usually another dictator) bent on overthrowing the incumbent ruler. Each side could furnish its client with money, weapons, materiel or advisors, but as soon as one side sent troops of its own, the other was precluded from doing so—because a direct conflict between America and Russia would have amounted to World War III, which is precisely what the Cold War had been designed to prevent. For the same reason, neither country could attack the other's ships or planes even when they were being used to supply a client state or faction and may thus have been prolonging a limited war indefinitely. Above all, the rules prohibited belligerents from employing the most effective weapons in their arsenals, nuclear bombs, which are reserved for total war and could mean the end of everything. Restrictions such as these are what make a limited war so difficult to win.

To a certain extent, the non-rich majority also profits from war. Some may work for a government contractor or for the government itself. Others may run small establishments catering to service personnel. The value of their homes and even their livelihoods may depend upon the presence of a military base nearby.

The benefits they receive, however, must be weighed against the costs, for they are the ones who most often pay the highest price of war, namely, their lives or those of their children. Accordingly, the rulers feel it necessary to publicly state reasons for going to war that are better than the real ones. We are fighting, they explain, to make the world "safe for democracy" (even though we may be supporting a brutal dictator who kills his political opponents or puts them in tiger cages) or to "defend American freedom" (but if we don't, we could go to jail for draft evasion) or to protect "our way of life" (i.e., to go on arrogating a disproportionately large share of the world's resources for our own use). At least it sounds good, and many of us will believe it because we want to. Our leaders are forcing us to go to war anyway, so we might as well imagine that we're doing it for some worthy cause.

Those of us who cannot swallow the official propaganda about what we're fighting for may at least agree about what we're fighting against. People were and still are divided in their opinions of Roosevelt and Churchill; a scant few have some nice things to say about Stalin; but no one in his right mind would stick up for Hitler. So universally abominated is this man that our leaders can count on the mere mention of his name to rally support for their own causes. All they have to do is find a substitute for Hitler.

It's only logical that capitalistic rulers should choose their communistic enemies to stand in for Hitler: Stalin of Russia, Mao Zedong of China, Kim Il Sung of North Korea, Fidel Castro of Cuba, Ho Chi Minh of North Vietnam, Daniel Ortega of Nicaragua, Mohammad Najibullah of Afghanistan, etc. (While predictable, their choices were nevertheless ironic—as Hitler himself was a rabid anticommunist.) The American people would willingly spend their blood and treasure on a war as long as they could be persuaded that the enemy was led by an equivalent of der Fuehrer. ("Fuehrer," by the way, is just a German word for "leader.")

With the Cold War drawing to a close, our own Fuehrers began to search beyond the communistic pale for a new Hitler whom both they and the Russian leaders could oppose in a joint effort to build a "new world order," administered by themselves, an order in which, as one of our leaders put it, "what we say goes!" Manuel Noriega of Panama and Saddam Hussein of Iraq were among the first to be chosen as the new Hitlers of the new world order.

There's more than one way to fight a war, but they all cost money. By spending billions of taxpayers' dollars on foreign aid, our rulers bribed the leaders of other countries to stay on our side and not join the Soviet bloc. In return for gratuities like these, foreign leaders commonly agree to vote with us in the U.N., to put their air space at our disposal and to allow us to occupy military bases and conduct espionage operations on their soil. (They don't always keep their promises, of course, but they wouldn't even bother to make promises unless their palms were being greased so thickly.)

The leaders of other countries would prefer not to grant us such privileges in the first place, but poverty often constrains them to act against their natural inclinations. Considered from either an individual or a group standpoint, the poor must serve the rich. And because the United States is wealthier than Russia, it has usually been able to outbid the latter for the favors of poor nations.

In their rivalry to dominate the world, the United States and the Soviet Union overextended themselves. American business owners grew rich by filling government contracts, while the government itself ran up a multi-trillion-dollar debt that eventually must be discharged by American taxpayers (most of whom are not rich). To help finance its annual budget deficit, the government sold bonds to foreign investors, thus selling the taxpayers into bondage to new masters from overseas. The Chinese say that "those who borrow, sell their freedom," but American politicians managed to sell other people's freedom for the money they borrowed: As an American earns enough dollars to pay his taxes, he is working for foreign masters as well as domestic ones.

The Russians fared even worse, for by the end of the Cold War they could hardly find anyone who even wanted to become their masters. Having trouble just feeding themselves, let alone continuing to support satellite nations, they could not persuade enough wealthy foreigners to invest in industries—and a work force—that had been worn out by a 40-year arms race that only private entrepreneurs (the "merchants of death") could win. In sum, both the U.S.S.R. and the U.S. had to pay an exorbitant price to become the world's leading superpowers. ("When you're the boss, you must pay the cost.")

But then, nothing is free. Everything costs something, if only the energy required when using it. (Even air must be drawn into the lungs before its oxygen can enter our bloodstream.) Regardless of the Consumer Price Index, the cost of living is always high.

First, a human being feels a lack. Next, he feels a desire for what he lacks. He then works to obtain the object of desire, that is, whatever he thinks will fill the emptiness he feels within himself. Whether the object is a practical necessity like food or something as frivolous as a bubble-gum card, the subject knows that he wants it. In attempting to satisfy desires, he normally encounters problems of some sort.

The main problem is scarcity. There is simply not enough to go around. Desiring subjects outnumber desirable objects. Human wants and needs exceed the Earth's capacity to satisfy them. From humanity's standpoint, the world is insufficient.

Scarcity leads to competition, and competition would almost always lead to war if it weren't for the intervention of governments. Governments are established to mediate the struggle for existence among the members of their respective societies. Without them, societies themselves could not exist.

The primary task of government is to keep order. This it does by enacting laws and having its servants enforce them. In the process, it provides businesses with the security they need to produce, distribute and exchange goods. That is why the leaders of business are so willing to pay bribes (i.e., make campaign contributions) to the leaders of government. The very existence of government allows people to acquire more wealth—or to hold on to what they already have.

Of almost equal importance is the government's responsibility for producing money. Government, in fact, controls the entire monetary system, selecting the standard unit of value, issuing currency, storing gold and silver bars, controlling interest rates, regulating the money supply, etc. In the most fundamental way, government is the real moneymaker of every society. Government may not be able to create wealth, but it can crank out currency (which is a much faster and easier means of exchange than barter).

To one extent or another, government regulates the economy itself. It may oversee the activities of both business and labor. The degree to which a government performs this regulatory function determines the economic system of its society: capitalist, communist or something in-between.

In return for the money and services provided by government, its subjects pay taxes. Those who complain that they must give too much money to the government seem to forget where they got it. If there were no government, there would be no money, or, at the very least, money would cease to have value.

Taxation is theft. To steal is to take from a person something that he does not want to give, and few people wish to give the government their tax money. Most of them do everything they can to pay the least taxes possible, and if they have the opportunity to pay none at all, they seize it without compunction. (Nonpayment of taxes is a privilege customarily reserved for those who are poor enough to lack income and assets or those rich enough to afford lawyers and accountants able to find sufficient loopholes for them.)

Paying taxes to the government is a lot like paying protection money to the mob. You don't want to do it, but if you don't, you'll be sorry. The average Joe would just as soon receive the protection and ancillary services provided by government without having to foot his share of the bill for them.

In every society, there is an eternal conflict between citizens who want to receive government services without paying taxes and, on the other side, politicians who desire to collect taxes without providing services. (Who, if anyone, will win this contest is impossible to predict, but one thing is for sure—even if nobody had to pay taxes anymore, people would still complain that they didn't get enough government services.)

Most people are too busy pursuing the almighty dollar to take part in public affairs. They leave politics to the politicians so that, when things go wrong, they can blame it all on their elected officials. ("Throw the bums out!") Replacing one set of bums with another, though, does not solve the problem. Just like their predecessors, the new bums must cater to the special interests whose monetary contributions made it possible for them to be elected.

Politicians solicit money from the rich and votes from the poor by promising to protect each from the other. The rich finance politicians, while the poor elect them. (If money alone were enough to win elections, Nelson Rockefeller would have been the 36th President of the United States—or at least the 37th.)

In return for the wages paid by their bosses, employees perform labor. The wealth of the ruling class is produced by the labor of the ruled class, just as the power of the rulers can be traced to the obedience of those they rule. (Economic necessity may impel some people to turn to crime, but it forces most of us to obey the law.)

The military might and thus the political power of a nation are measured by the number of soldiers and police officers on whom it can rely to enforce its proclamations. In like manner, its economic strength depends upon how many workers are available to produce its goods and how many consumers are waiting to buy them. (The more slaves they have, the wealthier the masters will be.)

The more wage slaves an employer has, the less he has to pay each one of them. The more voters there are, the less each vote counts. Therefore, it is not surprising that rulers, as a rule, encourage population growth in their domains.

Since the world does not have enough for everyone, governments must find ways to allocate scarce resources among subjects. The rulers could distribute everything equally, in which case everyone would be equally deprived. Or they could let some people enjoy a surplus while others suffer from a deficiency. (Either way, someone's going to be unhappy.) For the express purpose of resource allocation, a number of different economic systems have been devised.

One of the most popular (at least in theory) is laissez-faire capitalism. Also known as "free enterprise" because the participants in such an economy are free from government control, this system requires that the means of production be privately owned. It is the economic equivalent of democracy insofar as the voter is supposed to be sovereign. In a capitalist economy, the consumer casts dollar "votes" for his favorite products, thereby motivating business owners (who desire profits and fear losses) to produce more of these goods.

The consumer feels a desire for some product after suffering from a perceived lack thereof. If he has enough money to purchase the desired item, he can generate an effective demand for it. Business owners endeavor to meet consumer demand by paying workers to produce a sufficient supply of commodities. The difference between what it costs business owners to manufacture an item and the price at which they can sell it to consumers equals their profit. Demand (the desires of consuming subjects) elicits supply (the production of desired objects by business through labor).

Capitalism is supposed to stimulate healthy competition. In their competition to possess scarce goods, consumers drive up prices. In their efforts not to be undersold by each other, rival producers keep their prices below what they would actually prefer to ask. Each person is at liberty to buy anything he wishes, to produce whatever he thinks will yield the greatest profit or to take the job that pleases him most. One's prospects are limited only by one's industry and intelligence. The best thing about capitalism is that, under this system, everyone has an equal chance to succeed.

The worst thing about capitalism is that it really doesn't work that way. Free enterprise is not exactly free. In fact, it's so expensive that rich people are sometimes the only ones who can afford it.

Whether they got their money through hard work, cheating, inheritance, marriage, family connections or dumb luck, rich people are able to make substantial investments that hold the promise of big payoffs in the future; poor people, in contrast, barely have enough to hang on from one day to the next. Without needing to incur large debts, the rich can send their children to prestigious universities where they will be groomed for executive positions; the poor consider themselves fortunate if they can give their children enough schooling to qualify them for anything beyond menial jobs. By making hefty campaign contributions, people who have wealth can acquire the kind of political influence that is denied to those who lack such resources. In short, poor people cannot compete successfully with rich people in either business or government, as the rich can buy all the advantages they need to win out over all would-be competitors.

Competition, in the traditional sense of the word, is a thing of the past. In the good old days of sole proprietorships, each person had a fairly equal opportunity to launch his own business and capture his own small share of the market. But when the demands of mass production and mass markets began to call for ownership and control on a grand scale, the game was limited to a few key players—the major corporations of today. The owners (stockholders) of these corporations are so numerous that, for practical purposes, they must surrender virtually all operating control to their managers (the directors and officers). Small businesses now operate only on the margin of the American economy, and their chances of success are only marginal—while big business occupies a relatively secure position at the center of economic life. No enterprising newcomer (not even one armed with a biz-ad degree) would be wise to start his own auto-manufacturing firm in the hope of competing with the Ford Motor Company, unless, that is, he could obtain a $1,500,000,000 loan guarantee from the federal government as Lee Iacocca did in 1979. (Of course, Mr. Iacocca was CEO of the Chrysler Corporation when he got his bailout; 30 years later, the faltering Chrysler and General Motors were given much larger bailouts because they were supposedly "too big to fail," implying that other businesses may be too small to succeed.)

Competition between businesses implies waste. If two or more firms make the same product, they are wasting energy (through duplication of effort) and precious resources that could be pooled jointly. Everyone knows a lot of trees have to be cut down to publish books, newspapers and magazines, but few stop to think that the manufacturing of plastics requires coal, water, limestone, salt, gas and other natural resources, even though plastic products are "synthetic."

The demand for products, plastic or otherwise, can be synthetic as well. All too often, consumer demand is manufactured on Madison Avenue, where advertisers know how to arouse desires that would otherwise lie dormant. These advertising executives, masters of psychology one and all, are able to persuade the public to buy goods that it never even heard of before, much less pined for. Advertising can create demand where none existed, thus putting a new strain on the world's resources, which, unlike human desires, are severely limited.

In the theory of laissez-faire capitalism, the government adopts a hands-off policy regarding business, but in the real world, government and business work hand in hand to attain their common goals. President Theodore Roosevelt created the U.S. Department of Commerce for the purpose of curbing the excesses of big business; however, it evolved into an agency dedicated to making big business even bigger by providing services, information and even financial aid ("welfare for the rich"). "The business of America is business," declared President Calvin Coolidge; he went on to define the respective roles of masters and slaves when he said that "the man who builds a factory builds a temple ... The man who works there worships there." Andrew Mellon, Secretary of the Treasury under Presidents Coolidge, Harding and Hoover, opined that "the Government is just a business, and can and should be run on business principles." Before assuming office as President, Dwight D. Eisenhower's Secretary of Defense, General Motors president Charles "Engine Charlie" Wilson explained that he foresaw no conflict of interest between his business and government activities because, in his view, what is good for GM is good for the U.S.A. Another Eisenhower appointee, Secretary of the Interior Douglas McKay, observed astutely, "We're here in the saddle as an Administration representing business and industry." Apparently, the saddle wasn't big enough for the "nine millionaires and a plumber" who made up Ike's Cabinet, as the plumber (Secretary of Labor Martin Durkin) had to dismount after only eight months—when it became clear to him that he could never persuade the Administration to cooperate in revising legislation that had crippled labor unions for years. Secretary Durkin learned the hard way that elected officials (at least the Republican ones) aim to please business owners—which is understandable, since it was the money donated by businesses that helped those officials to be elected in the first place. (Meanwhile, affluent labor unions contribute money and volunteers to Democrats.) To show their gratitude and to protect the interests of rich people at home and abroad, politicians have always been willing to do almost anything—even if it meant sending poor people off to war.

As a way to order the economic affairs of life, a system far more rational and humane than capitalism is communism. Under communism, the community as a whole owns the means of production, and every member of it has an equal share. Scientific central planning would replace the anarchic production so wasteful of resources in a capitalist economy. Before long, nation-states would "wither away," leaving a worldwide "classless society" in which each person would give what he could and take what he needed. Poverty and injustice would fade from memory. Crime and war would likewise disappear, because there would no longer be any reasons for them to exist. Among master plans to build a better world, communism is unsurpassed for the beauty and nobility of its aims. There is only one thing wrong with it.

It doesn't work.

Stories and legends are told of how communism (at least in a primitive form) has been practiced by small societies based on agriculture, hunting or food gathering. If these tales are true, they demonstrate that this system might be viable for groups in which economic relations are simple and the potential for conflict can be held to a minimum. But anyone who imagines that communism is suitable for the millions living in an urban industrial society would be the type of person who believes in Santa Claus. (And, come to think of it, Karl Marx even looked like Santa!)

Communist theory assumes incorrectly that each member of a group will work for the common good and not his own. It presupposes that human beings are by nature generous and unselfish. (A five-year-old knows better than that.) Without the profit motive or the opportunity to serve their own private interests, most people have no compelling incentive to exert themselves. (As Soviet factory hands used to say, "They pretend to pay us, and we pretend to work.")

Capitalism, on the other hand, is founded upon the reality of human avarice. It takes heed of greed. It recognizes that, in the absence of a common enemy, the majority of people would rather compete than cooperate with each other. They don't want to have the same as everyone else—they want more.

The glaring disparity between haves and have-nots is tolerable as long as poor people think that they or their offspring have a chance (however remote) of amassing fortunes themselves. They don't want to lick their exploiters—they want to join them. ("I'll get mine, and to hell with you and yours!") So the poor minority goes on laboring for the rich majority, believing that someday its patience and industry will be rewarded.

Capitalist theory paints a picture of the human race that is dark, unflattering and accurate. As an economic system, capitalism itself is callous and cynical—but at least it works better than communism.

Capitalism works well for the rich and poorly (if at all) for the poor. In a free enterprise system, the distribution of wealth is not equal ... but then it was never meant to be. Happiness for some means unhappiness for others. For every winner, there must be at least one loser, and there are usually millions. More and more of a nation's wealth tends to be accumulated by less and less of its population, as some live in mansions while others sleep in cardboard boxes.

But the poor need not fear that the rich will eliminate them. On the contrary, the poor have always outnumbered the rich by a wide margin, and that margin will surely continue to widen. ("For the poor always ye have with you...") The rich need the poor, because masters always need slaves.

Q. Who's going to fight the wars, pound the beats, work the mines, till the fields, toil in the factories, collect the garbage and empty the bedpans?
A. Not the rich!

In every society, many disagreeable tasks have to be performed. These jobs are boring, unpleasant and/or dangerous, but they need to be done and the poor are elected.

The division of labor, or specialization, began with the distinction between master and slave. The slave was supposed to do the work, and the master made sure that he did. Throughout history, countless variations have been made upon the basic relationship of master and slave, for example, those of parent and child, chief and tribesman, king and subject, aristocrat and peasant, lord and vassal, landowner and serf and employer and employee. Typically, the master is rich and the slave is poor, at least in relation to one another. ("We live by the 'golden rule': Those who have the gold make the rules.")

Social stratification accompanies the division of labor. Who you are is determined in large measure by what you do. High-level positions and salaries are badges of rank in the socioeconomic hierarchy. (Ironically, the most essential jobs are often the lowest-paying. A political consultant, for instance, normally makes much more than a garbage collector—yet we could do without the former a lot longer than we could without the latter.)

There is one main difference between the poor and the rich. Poor people have to work for a living; rich ones don't. It doesn't matter how many necessities or even luxuries a person can afford. Arbitrary income levels are likewise irrelevant. A person is rich only if he does not need to work for someone else. Otherwise he is a slave to employers, customers or clients. No one is free when he has to work for a living.

A great deal of confusion surrounds the class structure of society, and, for the most part, the notions of upper, middle and lower classes cause the confusion. For centuries in Europe, aristocrats comprised the upper class; business owners, the middle class; and laborers, the lower class. Because Article I, Section 9(8) of the United States Constitution outlaws titles of nobility, American politicians and business owners (or at least the most successful among them) were once the only ones eligible for membership in the upper class of their country. Unemployed or underpaid laborers remained on the bottom. Those between the two extremes knew that they lacked the price of admission to the upper class, but they still wanted to feel that they were on a higher plane than the other members of the lower class; and so small-business owners, professionals, line managers, petty bureaucrats, white-collar workers and unionized blue-collar workers were unofficially lumped by social commentators into the "middle" class, which was further divided into "upper-middle" and "lower-middle" subclasses. Modern society, then, contains actually only two classes, but three or even four classes are falsely promised to us.

There are the ruling (or upper) class and the ruled (or lower) class. The upper class depends upon the lower class for labor and/or taxes, while the lower class depends upon the upper class for everything else. Directly or indirectly, members of the lower class work for those in the upper class. If they stopped doing so, they could no longer afford even the basic necessities, let alone the frills and status symbols that are prized by the more highly paid workers as outward and visible signs of their superiority to those on the very bottom of the heap. A higher standard of living does not necessarily produce a higher status in life. The "middle class" is a myth, propagated by capitalist society to pacify its laborers and to immunize them against communist propaganda.

Somebody has to be poor enough to do the dirty work. If a society does not have a lower class of its own, it must rent one from another society. In oil-rich Kuwait, for instance, where a multi-billionaire dictator could afford to give his subjects so many freebies that they didn't need to work, paupers had to be imported from countries like Jordan, Egypt and the Philippines just to handle the drudgery. (That's right—Arabs with Filipino houseboys!) After their country was invaded by Iraq, Kuwaitis were even able to employ American soldiers to do their fighting for them.

In a truly communist society, no one is rich or poor. There are no masters or slaves. Everyone is equal. But most people don't want to be equal. They want to be superior, and that's why communism can't succeed.

Communism didn't really fail in the U.S.S.R. It was never even attempted there. As described by Marx, communism is the final stage of a historical process that begins with a revolution and culminates in a classless, share-the-wealth society in which the government has withered away. During the transition, a dictatorship of the proletariat is instituted purely as a stopgap measure. But Russia stopped at the stopgap, leaving its proletarian dictatorship intact between the revolutions of November 1917 and December 1991.

Of course, critics could argue that Russia's dictatorship was never very proletarian. Before they became revolutionaries, Lenin had been a lawyer; Trotsky, a writer; and Stalin, a divinity student (!?). The rulers of the Soviet Union talked a lot about capital and labor, but few of them ever had any capital—and even fewer ever did any labor. A typical Soviet leader promised to do everything for the working stiff except become one.

Not that Americans have any reason to be smug. Our economic system has created problems of its own: recessions, depressions, the savings-and-loan crisis, bank failures, housing bubbles, financial fraud, predatory lending, unemployment, an annual budget deficit, a quarterly trade deficit and the national debt, just to name a few. As burdens multiply and opportunities dwindle, the outlook becomes increasingly bleak. But at least capitalism does not have to take the blame for our troubles, since the United States is no more a capitalist country than the Soviet Union was a communist one (even before the momentous events of August 1991).

To be sure, some elements of capitalism are present in the U.S. economy, just as elements of communism could be found in the U.S.S.R. for 74 years. America may be called "capitalistic" rather than capitalist, in the same way that Russia could have been referred to more aptly as "communistic" than communist. What prevents America from being fully capitalist is the same thing that kept Russia from being truly communist—in a word, government.

A government is not even supposed to exist in a communist society. In a capitalist one, it is not supposed to interfere with the economy. Adam Smith, one of capitalism's most famous exponents, believed that an "invisible hand" guides the economic affairs of individuals, each of whom acts to promote his self-interest. But that hand is far from invisible in the United States, whose government has habitually interceded on behalf of business. Not until the Great Depression threatened to ruin everything did the government begin in earnest to take the part of labor as well, providing welfare for the poor to counterbalance the welfare it had already been giving the rich.

"Liberal" or "progressive" thinkers tend to support government spending in general, while "conservatives" favor aid only to the rich. Both lines of thought are skewed.

The major problem faced by liberals is that of reproduction. If government starts to feed just one impecunious couple, it may wind up having to feed all their children, grandchildren and great-grandchildren. Population expands in direct proportion to the supply of food available, thus ultimately dooming such charitable efforts before they've even begun.

What conservatives tend to overlook is the interdependence of people living in a group. If it's every man for himself, then what's the point of having a society in the first place? Rich people would answer that societal law and order are needed to secure their lives, property and privileges, but poor people would probably not find that reason convincing enough, since their taxes (and labor) purchase most of that security.

To prevent the collapse of business, liberals grudgingly support government subsidies for the rich, and conservatives are willing to write off aid to the poor as premiums paid to insure the country against revolution. Both sides see that such expenditures are necessary, but neither should dare to call them capitalist or even capitalistic. On the contrary, they are socialistic.

Socialism is a cop-out. The socialist cannot make up his mind whether he is a capitalist or a communist, so he tries to be both at the same time. He desires to nationalize or at least to regulate major industries, BUT he doesn't want to abolish the institution of private property as such. He plans to redistribute wealth by means of taxation, BUT he does not envision a society in which each person receives an equal income. He would like his proposed reforms to take effect in the near future, BUT he sees no need for an immediate revolution. You can tell the socialist that he's trying to have things both ways, BUT it won't do any good, because he's already made up his mind.

Much of the New Deal legislation was socialistic in character. Declared unconstitutional in 1935, the National Industrial Recovery Act of 1933 led to the establishment of business codes governing wages, working hours and product quality. The Banking Act of 1933 set up the Federal Deposit Insurance Corporation (FDIC), which insures bank deposits and makes rules concerning the kinds of loans its member banks can grant. The Agricultural Adjustment Act was passed in 1933 to provide for the centralized planning of farm production. The year 1933 also witnessed the creation of the Tennessee Valley Authority, a federal project that contemplated nothing less than the physical and economic reconstruction of an entire river valley encompassing parts of seven states. Under the Securities and Exchange Act of 1934, a special commission (the SEC) would regulate the stock market. The Federal Housing Act of 1934 allowed the government to insure private lenders against losses on home mortgages. The National Labor Relations Act guaranteed workers' rights to union membership and collective bargaining when Congress passed it in 1935. In the same year, the Social Security Act paved the way for public pensions, unemployment compensation, disability allowances and financial aid to the needy. The Fair Labor Standards Act of 1938 established minimum wages and maximum hours for the nation's workers.

President Franklin D. Roosevelt always insisted that he had proposed these and other measures in order to save "the system of private property and free enterprise," as well as "our form of government." In any event, the effects of the New Deal are being felt to this day.

Taxes remained low until World War II forced the United States Government to raise money on an unprecedented scale. Beginning in 1940, a series of "revenue acts" boosted both proportional, normal income taxes for the average wage earner and progressive surtaxes for the wealthy. Progressive income taxes (combined with estate, gift, inheritance, capital-gains, corporate and excess-profits taxes) function to make Americans a little less unequal to each other. Of course, they don't go far enough for socialists like Norman Thomas, but they're still a long way from the ideals of such arch-conservative capitalists as Andrew Mellon, who held that rich people (like himself) should be exempted from taxation altogether. America isn't really a socialist country, but it's not exactly a capitalist one either.

In fact, the U.S. economy is a number of different systems patched together into one crazy quilt. Whenever private citizens or business firms endeavor to acquire wealth, they behave in a capitalistic manner. When the government grants aid to labor, it exhibits socialistic tendencies. When it helps business, it displays mercantilistic ones. No wonder economists like to say that America has a "mixed economy," though mixed-up would be more like it.

But Americans can always console themselves with the thought that Russia's economy is even more mixed-up. If, like America's, it is a patchwork of several systems, then even the patches are difficult to identify. Before glasnost (a proposed openness or transparency on the part of government), Soviet leaders always maintained that they practiced socialism merely as an interim measure to be adopted between the overthrow of the Czar and the advent of full-fledged communism. The government's ownership and control of all productive resources lent at least superficial support to the claim of socialism. If the government exists to serve the people, socialism prevails; but if the people exist to serve the government (as the markedly higher living standards of government officials would seem to suggest), then state capitalism is the rule. Russia's black market is an example of private capitalism. When we try to classify the economic system of Russia, about the only thing we can definitely rule out is communism. The Russian people may have abolished the Communist Party, but they cannot abolish communism because they never had it to begin with.

Less than four years after the Bolshevik Revolution, Lenin himself had begun to lose faith in communism. As agricultural and industrial production fell to a fraction of what they had been before the revolution, millions of Russians went hungry or starved to death. Desperate, Lenin inaugurated his "New Economic Policy," an experiment in free enterprise that permitted private citizens to produce and sell goods on the open market. The experiment failed. It took Stalin's despotic "Five-year Plans" to elevate his country to the rank of a major industrial power.

Perestroika (the restructuring of Russian society), then, is nothing new. It's as old as the New Economic Policy announced in 1921. Capitalism in Russia flopped many decades ago, and there is no reason to believe that it will work today. (If it does, however, the Russians can only hope that their economy will fare better than our own has been doing lately.)

In addition to the Cold War, the United States and the Soviet Union were locked in a struggle to see whose economic system was superior. ("We will bury you.") America now claims victory in this battle, even as its own economy is having serious problems.

With its booming GDP, the People's Republic of China may soon claim economic victory over the United States. Even if it does, however, its leaders would be disingenuous to claim that their win signifies the triumph of communism over capitalism. Although they cling sentimentally to their old moniker of the "Communist Party," they have achieved their success through pragmatic private enterprises rather than idealistic five-year plans, great leaps forward or cultural revolutions. By appealing to their subjects' profit motives, the Chinese rulers are in the process of beating capitalistic America at its own game.

But whether the contenders in the economic rivalry are capitalists or communists or something else altogether, at least it's nice to know that China, America, Russia and most other industrialized nations of the world have been able to produce at least one thing together—

Pollution. It poisons our air, water and soil; contaminates fish and wildlife; and may help raise the temperature of the Earth. It even punches holes in our atmosphere, through which the sun threatens to roast us alive with ultraviolet radiation.

Q. So what are we doing about it?
A. Creating more pollution, of course.

We burn more and more fossil fuels and increase our consumption of the very goods whose manufacture results in the emission of pollutants. Meanwhile, our elected officials pass laws to protect the environment and then gut them with amendments designed by business owners to whom they owe so many favors. Tree-hugging environmental activists protest loud and long, but unless they walk to the sites of their demonstrations, they too are part of the problem they wish to solve, for the hydrocarbons, carbon monoxide and nitrogen dioxide from their vehicles' exhaust is helping to pollute the planet they love so dearly.

None of us really wants to rape Mother Earth, but we just can't help ourselves. Whether we like it or not, pollution is inseparable from "our way of life." Pollution is the inevitable waste matter of civilization.

For most of their history and all of their prehistory, human beings lived off nature as they found it. Without technology, our primitive ancestors were easy prey to diseases, wild beasts and natural disasters. They hunted, fished and gathered vegetation until they were able to develop agriculture and animal husbandry. They made clothes with animal skins and later with cloth woven from wool, silk or cotton. They fashioned their weapons from stone, bronze or iron. After leaving the trees and caves, they built their homes using clay, wood or stone. At first, man adapted himself to his environment.

Then he began to adapt his environment to himself. In attempting to control nature, man changed the course of it. The trouble probably started when he learned how to make fire and thus release large amounts of carbon dioxide from wood into the atmosphere, laying the foundation for the "greenhouse effect" of today. When coal and oil became the fuels of choice, sulfur dioxide and nitrogen oxides as well as more carbon dioxide befouled the air—and "acid rain" began falling.

To supplement the normal chemical reactions occurring in nature, scientists learned how to induce chemical (and even nuclear) reactions of their own, rearranging the basic building blocks of matter and thereby creating some wholly new substances with unforeseen properties both benign and malignant. Chemicals such as methyl chloroform (an industrial solvent), chlorofluorocarbons

(CFCs, used in refrigerants, plastic foam, aerosol propellants, etc.) and halons (CFCs for fire extinguishers) ascend to the stratosphere where they perforate the ozone layer that shields us from most of the sun's ultraviolet rays—which can cause blindness and skin cancer.

Runoff carries pesticides, fertilizers, lead and mercury to the bottoms of bays and oceans. Toxic, infectious and nuclear wastes are all hazardous—even when they are dumped legally. Where nature once threatened to destroy the human race, the human race now poses a serious threat to nature and to itself as well, since it is an integral part of nature.

Pollution, then, is the unavoidable byproduct generated by the processing of natural resources into usable commodities. The process can be slowed and even altered somewhat, but it cannot be stopped. Pollution will surely worsen as world population and national economies continue to grow—no matter how efficient our technology becomes or how many international treaties we sign. The only alternative is to try turning back the clock to a pre-industrial era that is dead and gone and to which few people would wish to return, even if they could.

The Industrial Revolution, by accelerating the process of environmental modification, made possible the immense population of the world we live in. With the unlimited demands it places upon a limited world, that population is the root of pollution, poverty, oppression, war and every other evil that we face today. Of course, we are that population. The love of money is not the root of all evil—we are.

We can love money or we can hate it, but we cannot afford to be indifferent to it if we plan to go on living. As soft beings trapped in a hard world, we need many things in order to survive; and we need money to get the majority of those things. It's good that most people want money so badly, because it's a crime not to have it. We can be arrested for vagrancy or having "no visible means of support." (In the eyes of the law, it's a crime to be poor.) We only want what nature and society want us to want.

If we have enough money that we need not work for a living, then we are masters; if we don't, then we're slaves. Most people would like to have enough wealth to exploit their fellow human beings without being exploited in return. It is the dream of almost everyone to enslave everyone else.

Chapter 7: War and Peace

Life is not a war between good and evil. It is merely a conflict of interests.

Everyone has an interest in satisfying his own desires and allaying his own fears. If two or more people have the same desires, they may pursue the same object or else similar objects that are in short supply. Should one person fear what another desires, the fearful person may perceive the other person (as well as the object desired by the latter) as a threat. No two people's interests are exactly alike, and so they are bound to conflict with each other sooner or later. As long as there is more than one person in the world, war is inevitable.

All that is needed for war are two parties with opposing interests. We normally think of war in terms of international conflict. In a broader sense, however, it can just as easily be waged between different religious sects, tribes, clans, families or even individuals. War may come to fruition in a struggle between groups, but it germinates in the heart of the individual. Groups, after all, are nothing but collections of individuals. ("What if they had a war and nobody came?")

The individual is a world unto himself. The world exists solely through his perceptions of it, and it interests him only to the extent that it arouses desires and fears. In pursuing the objects of desire and fleeing from those of his fear, he encounters other individuals. If they get in his way, he perceives them as enemies to be overcome. Because each individual experiences the world in essentially the same manner, life becomes a war of each one against all others.

The only reason for individual combatants to cease their hostilities and form a group is so that they can align themselves against a common enemy. That enemy may be anything from hunger to insecurity to another individual or group. If the enemy is defeated, then the group may disband—in which case its members will go back to fighting among themselves. Uneasy alliances form, dissolve, re-form and shift as yesterday's enemies become today's friends and today's friends become tomorrow's enemies.

There are not enough good things in the world for everybody. Desiring subjects outnumber desired objects, and so someone has to do without. Scarcity leads to competition, and war is simply competition in the extreme.

In the absence of practical goals, people will fight each other for the sake of pure theory. Each person sees the world from his own limited viewpoint, but he wants to believe that his own view is absolutely correct and should be shared by everyone else.

Someone who is especially intolerant or insecure in his beliefs will do everything he can to force them on others. Even if he can find kindred spirits and unite with them, he still resents those outside his group for refusing to accept his views.

Throughout history, individuals and groups have shed blood just to prove who was right and who was wrong. Wars, particularly those involving religion, have often been fought over a mere difference of opinion.

The actual causes of war often belie the explanations given for it. National leaders are especially adept at giving official reasons for going to war that sound much better than the real ones. We are fighting, they say, to protect "freedom," when all they really want to do is make the world safe for Exxon oil slicks. Or else they tell us that we must defend our "strategic," "legitimate," "national" interests abroad. (How one nation can have a legitimate interest in another sovereign nation, they seldom bother to explain.) When they condemn rival leaders for "naked aggression," they are faulting their rivals for their failure to conceal their true war aims under the mantle of some high-sounding pretext. But any disinterested observer can see that all such pretexts are as transparent as the emperor's new clothes.

Rulers start wars because they want wealth, power or territory. But they hesitate to declare their objectives plainly, especially if they need the support of foreign rulers. To hold their alliance together, the allies will state their goals nebulously in an effort to reduce friction. If the alliance goes down to defeat, its promises won't matter anyway; but if it wins, then the strongest members can reap the greatest rewards, while those who profit least from the peace settlement can always complain that their noble war aims were betrayed.

People can find many reasons for going to war, but they really don't need any. War is the way of the world. The urge to fight may be observed in most young animals (including those of the human species). They're just doing what comes naturally when they struggle for dominance or for the sheer love of combat. The alternative for them would be boredom. War may be hell, but peace is dull.

Survival demands aggression, and this explains why aggressiveness is favored in the process of natural selection. One who keeps turning the other cheek will soon have no cheeks left. To accept an insult is to invite an injury, and to accept an injury is to invite annihilation.

Living things can survive only by killing other living things. Life needs more life for its sustenance. One species makes war on other species and also on itself, as the strong prey upon the weak. Big animals eat little animals. Even plants kill each other for water, minerals and sunlight. Nature sustains its existence by devouring itself and vomiting itself back, over and over again.

As usual, humanity changes the course of nature. Whether or not this change is for the better remains to be seen, but without it, human society would be impossible. Human rulers transform the natural war of each individual against all others into artificial wars between groups.

Governments stop wars inside their own jurisdictions and start them outside. Our leaders make it a crime for us to use violence against our fellow citizens—and a patriotic duty to use it against the citizens of other nations. We may hate and want to kill some people in our own country, but we're supposed to put aside our private quarrels and go marching halfway around the world, if need be, to kill people we haven't even met—just because their leaders have quarreled with our leaders.

If we have trouble whipping up the same enthusiasm for public wars that we have for our own private ones, our rulers are always ready to make speeches, wave flags and lead us in pledges and anthems calculated to make our patriotic blood boil. (And if that doesn't work, they can send us to jail for draft evasion, sedition or treason.) In any case, we can always count on our rulers to lay down our lives for their country.

Within its own borders, each country strives for peace. It never succeeds totally, but at least its rulers manage to hold violence to a minimum unless they preside over a failed state. This they accomplish by prescribing the rules of engagement according to the letter of the law. Wealth should be acquired through economic competition, inheritance, gambling or some other legal means; a business owner may cut prices but not his competitors' throats; if one person decides to rob or ruin another, then he must file suit or press charges against him. Private citizens should slap each other only with lawsuits, and they should hit nobody with anything heavier than an injunction.

Violence is the prerogative of the ruling class. The ruler doesn't steal money—he simply levies taxes and imposes fines. Instead of kidnapping anyone, he makes lawful arrests. And he never commits murder—he merely inflicts capital punishment.

The rulers can get away with what you and I would hang for, and that's why most of us walk the line that they draw for us. We wage our interpersonal wars according to the rules of civilized behavior ... because we know that, by using force on others, we run the risk of having our rulers use force on us.

Some are willing to take that risk. They are branded by society as criminals, and the name fits them well. For crime is, by definition, the infraction of law, and criminals are those who break the laws that our rulers made for us. Some criminals are proud, and they commit their crimes in order to defy authority. Others, who are stupid, simply make mistakes that they normally live to regret. A few are just plain greedy and feel that they deserve nothing less than everything.

But many criminals violate the law because they feel that they have to, that they have no other way to rectify the imbalance that exists between them and the rest of their society. If the severely underprivileged believe that they cannot get what they want in the "right" way, then they may try to get it any way they can.

For everyone to live in peace, everyone would have to be just. Each person, however, has his own idea of what is just, usually involving whatever promotes his own interests. Such ideas (and the people who hold them) are sure to clash with one another. Moreover, it is hard to be just in a world as unjust as ours, where the cruelest are often judged by both nature and society as the fittest to survive.

Hitler didn't want war. No national leader does, for war is risky, painful and expensive. Hitler would have much preferred to conquer the whole world without firing a single shot. He wished that every country could have been handed to him on a silver platter—as part of Czechoslovakia was at the Munich Conference of 1938.

All rulers want peace. They would be perfectly content to sit back and let everyone else satisfy their desires for them. But everyone else has his own desires, some of which conflict with those of the ruler. When people with such desires try to make their dreams come true, the rulers feel compelled to sic the police on their domestic opponents and the armed forces on their foreign ones.

As far as the rulers are concerned, it is their enemies at home and abroad who force them to use force. The rulers are not to blame—they feel—if some people will not do as they are told.

Most people will. They realize that the preponderance of force lies on the side of the rulers. Even if they own guns, private citizens are no match for the trained enforcers and sophisticated weaponry that the rulers have at their command—and that were paid for with citizens' tax money. (A .44-Magnum pistol or an AK-47 rifle cannot equalize a subject with a ruler who possesses an M1 tank or a B-52 airplane.)

The choices for most of us are simple. If our masters want us to labor for them, then we go to work or we go to the poorhouse. If they want us to fight for them, then we go to war or else to jail.

But we do not have to go far to go to war. War is not just one of those mass murders we read about in newspapers and history books. It is a part of our everyday life. (*C'est la vie; c'est la guerre: C'est la meme chose.*)

Every action is taken against something. Whether we lift soup with a spoon or boulders with a crane, we meet and try to overcome resistance in every phase of our active lives. One force opposes another, and the stronger prevails. This conflict cannot be avoided because it is the only way that energy can be transferred from one being to another.

War is more than simply a part of the natural or civic order. It is a precondition of life itself. Existence is the perception of an object by a subject. Where the subject ends, the object begins; and it is at the borderline between subject and object that conflict begins and spreads to other borders. Whenever lines are drawn between beings, the possibility of war is introduced. There would be no war if all were One. At the very least, it takes two to tangle.

The world is the battleground on which Being struggles against itself. Subject fights object in the arena of existence. No matter what side wins, Being loses. (In war, only death can be the victor.) For Being itself, existence is self-defeating.

Objects oppose objects, and subjects oppose objects without prejudice, but when subjects oppose subjects, things get personal. We love our friends because they help us to satisfy our desires and to allay our fears; we hate our enemies because they oppose our desires and arouse our fears.

Since our emotions are natural and spontaneous, they do not lend themselves readily to our conscious control. We can no more easily love our enemies than we can hate our friends. You cannot "love thy neighbor" just because someone tells you to. No law can even make us like each other.

Q. Why don't you make love, not war?
A. Because the one leads to the other.

Before anyone can make war, at least two people have to make love. In their relation to each other as sex objects, two subjects may unite to form a third subject. By reproducing themselves, lovers swell the ranks in the war of each against all. They also provide more soldiers for their rulers' wars against other rulers. The merchants of death manufacture the cannon, while the purveyors of life make the cannon fodder.

Individuals battle with other individuals, and the hostilities escalate as individuals form alliances against common enemies. Families make war on other families; tribes, on other tribes; clans, on other clans; and religious sects, on other religious sects. The conflicts with the biggest body counts are those fought between nations—but they all started because sometime, somewhere, at least two people loved each other.

Hitler was a baby once. He may have even been a cute one who filled his parents' hearts with joy. Whatever happened had to happen, yet it is tempting to speculate on what might have come to pass if Klara Polzl and Alois Schicklgruber had not made love to each other in 1888 (or any other year). Would the Germans have found themselves another Fuehrer, or could World War II have been averted entirely? (It's too bad we'll never have a chance to find out.)

Compromise is often suggested as an alternative to war, but it doesn't work for long. When neither party to a dispute can get everything he wants, both parties are dissatisfied. Their dissatisfaction lingers and grows until one side feels strong enough to go on the offensive. What we call "peace" is just a temporary lull in the fighting, a cease-fire used by the belligerents to marshal their forces in preparation for further combat.

Total surrender, if it were possible, would bring peace. As long as people followed the same leader and satisfied his desires alone, war would cease. (This was the dream of Hitler.) But each person has his own desires that he will satisfy first, given the opportunity. No one can totally surrender oneself to another.

And no one can totally win a war either. If you destroy your enemy once and for all, then your conquest is a dead one—since you thereby forfeit all rights to his labor. By sparing his life, on the other hand, you may enable him to rise up and conquer you someday. (Once the military master of Germany and Japan, America is now their economic slave—their debtor.) There is no lasting peace on this side of the grave.

The war of each one against all others will continue as long as the world does. It has to. Each person knows himself as both subject and object, but he can perceive everyone else only as an object. Because each and every subject can feel only his own feelings, he must put his own interests ahead of all others. War is the inescapable conflict of these opposing interests. (If my only choice is between you and me, then I have to choose me.)

"Blessed are the peacemakers," for "theirs is the kingdom of heaven." They could not possibly reign on Earth, where violence or the threat of it predominates. With tender hearts and noble sentiments, these ardent proponents of peace urge us to share when there is not enough to go around. They extol the virtues of cooperation, even though most people would prefer to savor the fruits of victory. By asking the impossible, they wage war against war. In effect, they declare war upon life itself. We can only hope that these worthy souls will find what they're looking for—at least in the hereafter.

In the here and now, though, anyone who's looking for peace is in the wrong world.

Chapter 8: Despair and Faith

Life requires faith, which is belief in an unproved assumption. ("Now faith is the substance of things hoped for, the evidence of things not seen." [Hebrews 11:1]) Without it, we would just lie down and die.

Most atheists have faith. Even if they do not believe in life after death, they generally believe in life after birth and act to preserve it. Infidels and true believers alike subscribe to what may be called the Four Articles of Natural Faith, which are as follows:

1. Life is worth living.
2. Desires are worth satisfying.
3. A law of cause and effect is in effect.
4. Life is worth reproducing.

That life is worth living has to be the first article of faith, for there is no better way to explain why people are ready to endure so much pain and frustration in order to stay alive. Even the easiest life is a hard one. In terms of aggravation alone, the cost of living is always high, and, no matter what their circumstances, most people are willing to pay that cost because they think it's worth it. They feel that life offers them the chance to obtain what they desire or to avoid what they fear (or both). They may never get what they want; but, until they draw their last breaths, they don't stop believing that they might get it.

Whether or not their desires are even worth satisfying is another moot point. If an individual never gets what he wants, then he never knows if his goal justified his effort. Should he attain his heart's desire and still not be satisfied, then he may conclude that the specific object of his desire, rather than the desire itself, was wrong. He should have become the president of the country, for instance, instead of the chairperson of the board. Even if he gets exactly what he wants, he will never have enough of it. The egoist will keep on acquiring and achieving for his own sake, while the altruist will try to help more and more of his fellow human beings—with no end in sight. Even a person bent only on survival must continue striving for the means to existence until he is no longer able to do so. To stop desiring would be to stop living.

We would not bother to strive for anything unless we felt that our efforts had a chance of producing the results we seek. Our actions, we believe, can serve as "causes" to bring about the "effects" we desire, and we base this assumption on our observations that A has repeatedly led to B in the past. Just because one thing follows another, however, does not prove that it follows from it. That something has happened in the same way yesterday and the day before yesterday does not necessarily mean that it will happen in the same way today, tomorrow or the day after tomorrow. Experience of the past is no guarantee of the future, yet we go on acting as if it were—and having faith that it is. (We have to, if we want life to go on.)

For human beings, reproduction is the ultimate act of faith. Nonhuman beings do not know that their sexual activities may cause the existence of new beings, but most human adults do. A baby is an incarnation of desire, embodying its parents' lust for life. By reproducing himself, a person expresses his approval of the world. It is good enough for his child, he declares by his action, as well as for himself. Except under unusual circumstances, a parent would be a hypocrite to say that life is not worth living.

No proof exists for the value of life, the worth of desires, the power of causation or the advisability of reproduction—but none is necessary. These are articles of faith, after all, the first three being required for the survival of the individual, the fourth for the continuance of the species. This is the only faith needed by some people to go on living in the world and to bring other people into it.

For others, this is not enough. They need to believe in something besides nature, something over and above it. Their faith in the supernatural usually takes the form of religion. While the world's religions are numerous and diverse, most of them include the following four articles in their respective canons:

1. God exists.
2. God is perfect, being Absolute, Infinite, undivided, all-good, all-wise and all-powerful.
3. Life is governed by a divine purpose.
4. There is life after death.

Existence is the perception of an object by a subject; and so, if God exists, He would have to be a subject or an object or both. Believers think of Him as a subject who sees all and knows all. In their view, He is also an object of worship to be venerated by everyone capable of doing so. He exists apart from His creation, yet He is somehow present in it.

In regarding the Supreme Being as perfect, human beings ascribe to Him those qualities that they prize most in themselves—goodness, knowledge and power. They believe that God cannot be anything but good, knowledgeable and powerful. To the minds of the faithful, He cannot do anything wrong or fail to do anything right. His perfection is without qualification or bounds.

If God's in His heaven, then all must be right with the world. God knows exactly why things happen even if we do not, and because He is all-good, everything must happen for the best. Providence rules the world and imparts a divine meaning to our earthly life.

Life would lose whatever meaning it had if it were to end. In that event, everything would come to nothing. A benevolent God, it is hoped, would not create beings in His own image just to obliterate them; and therefore faith demands an afterlife. In the light of faith, death is the end of only our mortal existence—and the beginning of an immortal one.

There is no more proof for these Four Articles of Supernatural Faith than there is for the Four Articles of Natural Faith—and no less either. Natural faith is required to preserve our bodies, while supernatural faith is often needed to comfort our souls. All faith is self-validating if it works for those who have it.

The teachings of religion cannot be refuted with mere words. Faith comes from the heart, not the head. Only a pseudo-intellectual would imagine that an Infinite Being could be subject to the rules of human thought.

Nevertheless, a faith that would require us to abandon completely our normal process of thinking would leave us unprepared to cope with the world that God made for us, where we need to keep our wits about us just to survive. If God gave us our intelligence, then He obliges us to use it. Because the Articles of Faith are so important to us, we must question those Articles even if we can never disprove them or would never wish to do so. And in the absence of a divine epiphany, the only revelation to which a human being can aspire is the truth that a human mind can reveal.

On the basis of our own definitions, we must assume that God's perfection precludes His existence. If God is either a subject or an object, then there is something that He is not. The subject ends where the object begins, whereas Godhead knows no limitations. He is the One and Only. If God were both subject and object, He would be divided into parts, but instead He must be at One with Himself. God is God, even though no subject can actually perceive Him as an object. ("I AM THAT I AM." [Exodus 3:14])

The Being of God cannot be seriously doubted. Being is the ground of existence, and God can be nothing less than Being Itself—perfect, indivisible and Absolute. (Existence cannot exist without Being, but Being can be without existence.) Absolute Being cannot participate in the relativity of existence: The Absolute cannot be relative any more than the relative can be Absolute.

There are many beings, but there is only One Being. God is, but He does not exist. God is God, but He does not exist as a god or as anything else in the world. This is only fitting, for imperfect beings belong in an imperfect world—while the perfect Being does not.

No body is perfect, and the world is made up of bodies, both animate and inanimate. If our own bodies were perfect, we would not have to suffer. Because they are finite and divisible, however, they are vulnerable to attacks by other bodies, both animate and inanimate.

God has no body. Being perfect (i.e., as perfect Being), He suffices in Himself. He is without beginning or ending, and He cannot be divided into parts. He cannot be perceived, let alone injured. He never grows cold or hungry, old or ill—and He doesn't even have to work for a living.

It is easy for God not to sin. He is under pressure from neither internal impulses nor external circumstances. Since He feels no pleasure or pain, He cannot have desires or fears in the way that we do. He is immune to the passions of love and hate. God is above good and evil, values that can be held only by subjects with bodies capable of being helped or hurt by other bodies.

Man cannot afford to be so indifferent. He loves and desires objects that give him pleasure and calls them good. He hates and fears objects that give him pain and calls them evil.

Because desiring subjects outnumber desired objects, the subjects bring evil upon one another while pursuing what they imagine to be their own good. Whether we want to or not, we often hurt others when we attempt to help ourselves. Try as we might, we cannot always get out of each other's way. Our desires compel us to do some things that we feel we shouldn't do, while our fears prevent us from doing things that we think we ought to do. On the day of his birth, each person begins to hurt others—and he does not stop until the day of his death. (If God forbade man to sin when thrusting him into the world, He might as well have thrown man into the ocean and ordered him not to get wet.)

Man is condemned to sin, whereas God is incapable of evil. While man is an imperfect, finite, relative being, God is the perfect, Infinite, Absolute Being. Man's natural faculties do not even permit him to apprehend the supernatural. As eagerly as he reaches for Heaven, his feet remain firmly planted on Earth. Man can have no communion with God, and the Absolute Being cannot relate to a relative being or to anything else. ("For my thoughts are not your thoughts/ neither are your ways my ways, saith the Lord." [Isaiah 55:8])

To bridge the gap between God and us, prophets volunteer their services. Prophets are people who claim to speak for God. In their roles as the middlemen between divinity and humanity, they have founded some of the world's foremost religions.

The prophet purports to know the divine truth about life and death. We should believe his teachings, he tells us, for the same reason that we accept logical deductions—namely, the authority that they are alleged to possess. The prophet's argument goes something like this:

God never lies or makes a mistake.
The prophet speaks for God.
Therefore, the prophet never lies or makes a mistake.

If we accept the premises of the prophet's argument, then we cannot reject his conclusion. His major premise is indisputable: Because God is all-good and all-knowing, He would never utter a falsehood or commit an error. It is the prophet's claim to be God's spokesman that raises a question in our minds.

If someone whom we knew personally were to tell us that he had just spoken with God, we would probably think that he was joking, drunk or mad. Why, then, should we give any more credence to people we have never met and who may have died hundreds or even thousands of years ago? (Of course, we might be more inclined to believe that these ancient prophets did represent the Almighty if they were still alive today.)

As evidence of their divine inspiration, prophets frequently adduce miracles or predictions ("prophecies"). Their ability to do things that a normal human being cannot do, they contend, proves that God is on their side. Miracles and prophecies serve as their credentials.

As supernatural events supposedly caused by God, miracles are either imperceptible or incredible. Human beings' natural faculties enable them to perceive only natural phenomena, however abnormal the phenomena may be.

Reports of miracles come mainly from the distant past, when people were not as familiar with the workings of nature as they are today. Much that is commonplace to us would have seemed miraculous to our ancestors. Even if a modern scientist could not explain an occurrence that he himself had observed, he would not call it a miracle for that reason. He should readily admit that he does not have all the answers and that science is an ongoing process of discovery. (His training, however, might lead him to suspect that whatever is physically possible is also natural.)

A true miracle would violate the laws of nature—which were presumably enacted by a perfect and immutable God. It is hard to believe that God would break His own laws merely for the sake of giving a testimonial to a human being. A magician may take our breath away, but he does not deserve our faith just because he can do a few tricks for us.

Prophecies are even less persuasive. As a rule, they are worded vaguely enough to fit a large number of possible outcomes. Even the fulfillment of a specific prophecy could be rightly attributed to guesswork or coincidence. When prophets make consistently accurate predictions in the sacred writings, they may owe their "prescience" less to divine afflatus than to revisions made by editors and translators long after the forecast events took place. Again, the number of years separating us from both the prophecies and the actual events makes any attempt at verification impracticable.

But even if we cannot give much credence to their credentials, we may find ourselves tempted to believe in the prophets themselves. From all accounts, the founders of the world's major religions were exceptional human beings, gifted in every important respect. They displayed vision, courage, integrity, brilliance and, most significant of all, charisma. Their magnetic personalities drew legions of faithful followers to them.

The prophet gives pleasure to his followers by satisfying their desire for a purposeful, everlasting life and by allaying their fear of death. Because he makes them feel good, they feel that he is good, and they come to love him for that reason. People believe what they want to believe, and they always want to believe someone they love. When the prophet declares that he speaks for God, his followers put their faith in him.

Religious people don't really believe in God. They believe in other people—people who claim to speak for God. Religions are sets of beliefs that human beings take for gospel from other human beings. And the followers of a religion are expected to have faith in more people then just the prophets. A lot more.

In ancient times, we are told, God (or one of His "angels") spoke to a prophet. The prophet then told his followers what he had heard (to the best of his recollection). If he did not record his message himself, this task had to be performed by his followers—perhaps years after his death; until then, the holy words were transmitted orally. The printing press would not be invented until the fifteenth century, and so the scriptures had to be written and rewritten by hand, using materials that were grossly deficient by today's standards. Scribes did their best to fill in gaps, correct previous errors and decipher illegible marks, but these scribes were only human. Those who attempted to translate their spiritual leader's words for the people of other cultures faced even greater difficulties, as they discovered that foreign languages did not always furnish them with the precise words they needed.

When the founder of a religion died, his followers needed a new leader. They began to organize themselves into groups (e.g., "churches") in order to combat what they saw as the false religions preached by other groups, and they recognized individuals within their own groups as "authorities" on their religion. These gurus, rabbis, priests, imams and other religious leaders took it upon themselves to decide which of the scriptures had been divinely inspired. Those that they selected found their way into the group's bible, while the rest were consigned to oblivion. The followers had only to believe the writings that their leaders chose for them—and only in the way that their leaders interpreted those writings for them. (Anything else would have been "heresy.") When the adherent of a religion says that he has faith in God, what he really means is that he has faith in the ability of his human leaders to correctly report, record, transcribe, translate, edit and interpret the Word of God for him.

On days when inclement weather prevents elementary school pupils from going outside for recess, their teachers will sometimes lead them in a game that can be played indoors. After arranging his charges in a circle, the teacher writes a short sentence on a piece of paper and shows it to only one of his pupils. If the message was "bears love honey," then the one who read it cups his hands over the left ear of the pupil on his right and recites those very words to him. The second pupil then does his best to repeat the message exactly to the third schoolmate in line, and the process continues until the message has come full circle. The last one in the circle (i.e., the one to the immediate left of the pupil who read the teacher's message) is asked by the teacher to tell the entire group what he has just heard. He usually responds with a phrase like "chairs cost money" or something even more dissimilar to the original message. Whether someone in the circle mistook or deliberately changed the words, the final result demonstrates that the people at the end of the line have no idea of what the people at the beginning of the line were told—until the teacher himself tells them.

In this instance, of course, the teacher is only playing a game with his pupils. Had he wished to convey an important message (such as a code of classroom behavior), he would have delivered it personally to his entire class. He would not have asked one pupil to pass it on to the others, for such a request would be unfair to both the pupil and his schoolmates.

If it takes less than three minutes for fewer than 30 people to distort a simple statement beyond recognition, just imagine what many thousands of people can do—in the course of millennia—to something as profound as divine truth. The prophet's disciples may have misquoted him. A scribe might have copied the wrong words, or the Word of God itself could lose something in the translation from the prophet's native tongue to a foreign one. Today, clergymen may be misinterpreting the scriptures. Even if the prophet himself was divinely inspired, that doesn't mean that any of his followers were. Some of them, at least, could have made mistakes or told lies.

So could the prophet. We have only his word, not God's Word, that he communicated with the Almighty. And anyone can claim to speak for God.

Jim Jones, Jim Bakker and Jim Swaggart claimed to speak for God. So did Pope Alexander VI, the unwed father (and mentor) of Lucrezia and Cesare Borgia. Even Adolf Hitler once proclaimed, "To serve Hitler is to serve Germany, and to serve Germany is to serve God."

Q. How can you tell the false prophets from the true ones?
A. Only God knows.

The original prophets appear to have been people of the highest moral caliber, and so we can probably feel safe in believing that they believed the things they said. But since God usually appeared to them in dreams or visions, the prophets themselves could have never been quite sure that the things they saw and heard resulted from divine inspiration or from something they ate. For that matter, these "revelations" could have been caused by something they didn't eat, as it was often their custom to fast for long periods in order to purify themselves for their encounters with God. By modifying their body chemistry and thus their mental functions, they were liable to see or hear almost anything.

An attack upon religion may be heresy, but then religion itself is founded upon hearsay. Religious leaders dispense a second-hand faith, adjuring us to accept uncritically what someone else has seen or heard: They expect us to believe that one person can understand divine truth and explain it to the rest of us. Religion is the faith not of man in God but of man in man.

Such faith is sadly misplaced, as men cannot help letting each other down. ("Thus saith the Lord: Cursed be the man that trusteth in man..." [Jeremiah 17:5]) For all their genius and virtue, the prophets could never have measured up to their task, since the limited mind of man cannot reflect the boundless mind of God. (Men most likely put words in God's mouth and then imagined that it was the other way around.) With their lofty spirits, the prophets towered over most of their fellow human beings, but they shrank to insignificance when compared with the Infinite Being.

God needs no middlemen: He is all-powerful, after all. God doesn't need messengers (prophets); anything He wants to say to us, He can say on His own. Nor does He need schools (churches), textbooks (bibles) or teachers (priests). Whatever we ought to learn, He can teach us Himself. Man may need God, but God does not need man.

Man needs God to sanctify himself. Without God, man is just another animal. Most people cannot bear the thought that while they may be cleverer than apes, they are essentially no better.

The devout person believes that he has an immortal soul. His soul, he feels, sets him apart from other animals and provides him with a link to God. Like God, though, the soul cannot be seen, heard, touched, smelled or tasted. The soul is another object of faith.

The human soul, hold the faithful, gives us a purpose in this life and a destiny in the next one. According to this view, God put us on Earth to serve Him. Our reward for faithful service will be a deathless afterlife of pleasure, while the punishment for disbelief and disobedience will be an eternity of pain.

To serve God is the most exalted vocation that anyone could ever pursue in this world. It is also the most futile. As the omnipotent Being, God has no use for servants—human, angelic or otherwise.

If God wanted anything, He could have it without any effort, just by desiring it. If He needed something done, He could do it Himself and better than anyone else could. But God is already perfect and Self-sufficient.

Q. What can you give to the man who has everything?
A. Nothing.

We have no reason to ask God for what we want, since He already knows what we need and will surely give us what is best for us. The perfect Being suffers from no emotional insecurity, and so praise is wasted on Him. It is pointless to confess our sins to the omniscient God. Prayer, worship and all other religious rites are useless for the purpose of serving God.

Man uses religion only to serve himself. Religion gives the leader a special authority to rule, and it provides the follower with a potent reason to obey. For both, it tenders the promise of an unlimited future.

Gurus, rabbis, priests and imams are not the only ones who claim a divine right to rule. Secular leaders like to assert the same prerogative. In his "Gospel of Wealth," Andrew Carnegie wrote that wealth is a blessing conferred by God upon His elect, an opinion shared by religious leaders no less notable than John Calvin and John Wesley. John D. Rockefeller stated that "the growth of a large business is merely the survival of the fittest ... the working out of a law of nature and a law of God."

During the anthracite-coal miner's strike of 1902, other business leaders endeavored to practice what Carnegie and Rockefeller had preached. Reading Railroad president George F. Baer, speaking on behalf of the mine operators, refused to negotiate with the United Mine Workers because, he reasoned, "God in His infinite wisdom has given control of the property interests" to corporations, not to labor unions.

Except in officially atheistic countries—and even in nations where church and state are legally separated—politicians often invoke the name of God when they go to war or otherwise commit their followers to some momentous undertaking. As the "King of Kings and Lord of Lords," the God of organized religion personifies the ruling class of society.

For the ruled class, disobedience is the original sin. All suffering results from man's refusal to do the will of God or of His human representatives. St. Paul eloquently describes the subject's duty to obey the rulers in a passage from the New Testament: "Let every soul be subject unto the higher powers. For there is no power but of God: The powers that be are ordained of God." (Romans 13:1) In the book of Ephesians, he goes on to say that slaves should serve their masters, wives should submit to their husbands and children should honor their parents. (Never mind if your ruler is a tyrant; your master, a brute; your husband, a wife beater; or your parent, a child abuser—just do what they tell you!) The cardinal virtue of devout people is their readiness to follow orders.

Most people are too preoccupied with their worship of the almighty dollar to bother questioning their rulers' fiats. Blind obedience saves them the trouble of deliberation. As a means to avoid making one's own decisions, faith is a comfortable substitute for thought.

The rulers, alas, cannot always justify the faith that their subjects place in them. Because they are less perfect than the God they claim to represent, rulers cannot help making decisions that are less than perfect. For causes that were supposed to be holy, they have led their followers into some decidedly unholy wars, crusades, inquisitions, pogroms, massacres and witch hunts. These man-made disasters can be attributed, at least in part, to the fact that the power of our rulers often exceeds their wisdom and their goodness.

Notwithstanding their power, though, earthly rulers cannot prevent natural disasters such as fires, floods, famines, epidemics, storms and earthquakes. They are unable to control these "acts of God," as they call them. (With a God like this, ask the heretics, who needs a Devil?)

Q. Why does God permit evil?
A. God permits everything that nature does not forbid. A human being calls things good or evil according to whether they give him pleasure or pain. Since God is impervious to pleasure and pain, He does not distinguish between good and evil.

In spite of their flaws, our leaders must be obeyed—or else. Even if we manage to defy our earthly masters with impunity, we shall not escape the wrath of our heavenly Lord. We can expect to pay for our transgressions in the next world, if not this one. The "powers that be" are "God's ministers" on Earth, explains St. Paul. "Whosoever therefore resisteth the power, resisteth the ordinance of God: and they that resist shall receive to themselves damnation." (Romans 13:2)

At the same time that God's spokesmen threaten us with their big stick, they entice us with a fat, juicy carrot. Anyone who doesn't do as he's told will go to Hell, but everyone who submits will go to Heaven. The sinner will endure everlasting torment, while the saint will enjoy an eternity of ... what?

Theologians can afford to be more specific about Hell than Heaven. They may safely assume that most people would not relish the prospect of living amid fire, brimstone and undying worms for a moment, let alone forever. It is not difficult to envision Hell, for many things that we experience on Earth could be a part of it.

Imagining what Heaven is like, however, is not as easy. The human mind cannot conceive of any single place where everyone could be happy. One person's Heaven would likely be another person's Hell. Besides, the most popular pleasures are physical in nature, and—even if they could be experienced by an immortal soul after the mortal body has perished——such sensual delights are generally regarded as sinful. Yet only the most pious could enjoy singing hymns and attending church socials after the first million years or so.

Preachers love to fixate upon the tortures of the damned. But when it comes to the joys of the blessed, they usually curb their tongues, preferring to describe Heaven in such hazy terms as "the peace of God, which passeth all understanding." (Philippians 4:7) Anyone who sacrifices his hopes of earthly happiness in return for admission to Heaven is, in effect, buying a pig in a poke.

Peace is Heaven, while war is Hell. Like Hell on Earth, Hell in Hell would be a war of each individual against all others. In Heaven, contrarily, there would be no enemies to defeat, no obstacles to overcome, no challenges to meet—and nothing to achieve. It would not take long to grow bored in Heaven.

Earthly life offers many opportunities to be perfectly miserable, but it never makes us perfectly happy. Pain or the threat of it always looms on the horizon. In an afterlife, Hell is supposed to be eternal pain without pleasure, while Heaven is supposed to be eternal pleasure without pain. As we saw in chapter 2, though, pleasure is simply the alleviation of pain; thus, there can be pain without pleasure, but there can be no pleasure without pain. Hell may well exist—at least on this side of the grave—but Heaven could never exist anywhere.

Pleasure, like life itself, is inseparable from pain. If there is an afterlife, it may be better than this life or it may be worse (or it may be more of the same); but it cannot be painless unless it is also pleasureless, even if it entails only the pain of boredom. (And an eternity of boredom would be more than painful enough.)

No one (whom we know personally) has returned from the next world to tell us about it, and so what it is—or even if it is—remains a question without an answer. But never mind that. It has always been humanity's fondest wish to live forever, and many people cling to it as tenaciously as they do to the instinct for self-preservation. If science, philosophy or common sense cannot promise them eternal life, then they will turn to religion. To get what they want, they will believe what they have to, even if they do not fully understand what they believe. (A person who has faith is willing to believe things that no one in his right mind would believe.)

Without question, God deserves our total faith and obedience. It would not be wise to trifle with a Being who could turn us into pillars of salt if He chose to. But even if we could safely ignore His power, we should still do His bidding. He's God, after all, and so He can't possibly be wrong about anything. (Indeed, if our opinion differed from His on any subject, then the mistake would have to be ours.) God has authority over the universe because He is the author of it. The world is His creation, and thus He must know everything there is to know about it.

If God appeared to St. Paul on the road to Damascus and ordered him to stop persecuting Christians, then Paul did well to obey. If God gave the 10 Commandments to Moses on Mount Sinai, then that man was responsible for observing the Decalogue. If God enjoined Abraham to slay Isaac, the patriarch was right to pull a knife on his own son. If God forbade Adam and Eve to eat the fruit from one of His trees in the Garden of Eden, the unhappy couple should have complied or else been prepared to face the consequences. (It is difficult to understand, though, why anyone else should have to atone for their sin.) And if God gives us an order, then we'd better follow it without hesitation.

But, seriously, when was the last time that God gave you an order? To be sure, lots of people have probably given you orders in the name of God, but anybody could do that. If you acceded to their wishes, you were putting your faith in man, not God.

The trouble with human beings is that they are only human. They have a tendency to err and to prevaricate. As St. Peter, the gatekeeper of Heaven, affirmed: "We ought to obey God rather than men." (Acts 5:29) Until God Himself tells us what to do, we're on our own.

A few religions attempt to eliminate the middleman. Their founder, at least, is alleged to be none other than God Himself or His offspring (or an incomprehensible combination of both). Their Deity, they maintain, once walked the Earth in human form, spreading the gospel Himself in words that human beings could readily understand and accept. In their effort to go straight to the source, such religions disavow any need for human intercessors.

This doctrine of the divine establishment of religion solves one problem resulting from the doctrine of divine inspiration, but it leaves all the others unsolved and creates some new ones as well. If God founds His own religion, a prophet cannot misquote Him; but His words can still be miswritten, miscopied, mistranslated, misinterpreted and misunderstood by His all-too-human followers after He has returned to Heaven. Even greater difficulties arise over the notion of the Divinity's assuming human form. ("It is believable because it is absurd. It is certain because it is impossible.")

God is God, and man is man, and never the twain shall meet—not even in an incarnation. If something looks like a man, walks like a man and talks like a man, we can probably assume that it is a man—especially if it dies like a man. An Infinite Being can do everything except become finite and remain Infinite. If God became man, then He ceased to be God.

Perhaps this is exactly what happened. In sinking to man's level, God may have fallen from His own. Man in the world could represent God fallen from Heaven, just as existence could be viewed as Being fallen from Its perfect state of nonexistence and shattered into the pieces of the world. By this interpretation, God cannot regain His Godhead without surrendering His manhood. He can be God or he can be man, but not even He can have it both ways at the same time. Being cannot reclaim Its perfection until It relinquishes Its existence.

The story of Jesus Christ can serve as a parable of Being and existence. When the Word was made flesh, It lost Its Divinity. The only way for Jesus to recover His perfect Being, as the Son of God, was to renounce his imperfect existence as the son of man. This he did on the cross, where he symbolized Being in the state of existence—finite, vulnerable and anguished. "My God, my God, why hast thou forsaken me?" he cried out in his agony, despairing completely of this "present evil world." When he finally "gave up the ghost," his suffering ended once and for all, and he rose again to that realm of pure Being (i.e., nonexistence) from which he and all of us have strayed at such a great cost.

In the Book of Revelation, St. John the Divine predicts the Second Coming of Christ. According to the prophet, Christ doesn't plan to be crucified again. This time he'll bring an invincible army of angels with him. He won't waste his breath preaching to unbelievers. Anyone who doesn't agree with him will be hurled into a pit of fire.

The Second Coming, as envisioned by St. John, signifies the complete despair of God—Who, being unable to convert the wicked, will destroy them utterly. He will have lost all faith in His own power to redeem the very beings He Himself created. Like so many prophecies, however, this one has not been fulfilled, and it never will be.

Shortly before the execution of Jesus, his disciples asked him when they could expect his return to Earth. He replied that, while he did not know the exact day or hour, "this generation will not pass away till" the Second Coming had taken place. (Matthew 24:34) Well, that generation passed away almost two thousand years ago, and it hasn't happened yet.

No matter how long we wait for him, Jesus won't come back. Dead people never do. They would be fools to return to life even if they could, since they are much better off as they are now. According to the wise King Solomon, who preferred death to all the money, power and sex that he had in life...

> A good name is better than precious ointment;
> and the day of death than the day of one's birth.
> It is better to go to the house of mourning,
> than to the house of feasting:
> for that is the end of all men;
> and the living will lay it to his heart.
> (Ecclesiastes 7:1-2)

Jesus has no reason to return, for he already accomplished his mission on Earth. Admittedly, the world is no better "A.D." than it was "B.C." In fact, it's a lot worse, since there are now a lot more people in it with a lot more problems. But even though Jesus could not save the world, he showed the world how to save itself, by "giving up the ghost." By despairing of life and having faith in death, each person can become his own messiah. "In the world ye shall have tribulation," said Jesus, "but be of good cheer; I have overcome the world." (John 16:33)

At the Crucifixion, Jesus encouraged one of his fellow victims to look forward to death, assuring him that "Today shalt thou be with me in paradise."

(Luke 23:43) Pleasure is the alleviation of pain, and so death—as the alleviation of all pain—seems heavenly indeed.

"[W]eep not for me," Jesus urged the female spectators bewailing his fate at Golgotha, "but weep for yourselves, and for your children. For behold, the days are coming, in the which they shall say, Blessed are the barren, and the wombs that never bare, and the paps which never gave suck." (Luke 23:28-29) In other words, he was advising women to be fruitless and stop multiplying. It may be better to die than to live, as Solomon remarked, but it is best not to be born at all. ("Cursed be the day wherein I was born: Let not the day wherein my mother bare me be blessed." [Jeremiah 20:14])

Existence allows Being to become conscious of Itself. Through the window of a living subject, the eye of Being sees itself reflected in the objects of the world, as if in a mirror. When the eye sees its own reflection in the mirror, the reflected eye looks right back at it. Existence enables God to be aware of Himself. Every subject perceives (and every object exhibits) a different aspect of God. In the aggregate, these perceived aspects amount to the world.

The world is Being in the state of existence. Here one Being has become many beings. There can be any number of objects to perceive in the world, but there must be at least one subject alive to perceive them. Life, then, makes existence possible.

God is Being in the state of nonexistence. As the One and Only, God is not a subject or an object or anything else. In fact, God is not even a "He," though we speak of the Supreme Being anthropomorphically because we value ourselves above all other beings. (And if worms believed in God, they would believe in an all-good, all-wise, all-powerful worm.) Pure Being, or God, does not exist because no living subject can perceive It. Pure Being precludes life, while life makes existence possible.

To God, a matter of life and death is a matter of indifference. It does not live and It cannot die. Whether the world goes on forever or ends tomorrow is of no consequence. Being will always be, even if existence ceases to exist. Because God feels neither pleasure nor pain, He makes no distinction between good and evil. God doesn't judge.

A human being has to. As one of God's subjects, he perceives objects in the world. He feels the pains and pleasures of living and the pain of dying—after which he feels nothing detectable. As opposed to other subjects, he discriminates between good and evil. Only humans have both the need and the capacity to decide whether life is worth living.

Humanity provides Being with Its clearest perspective on the world. Through the window of a human subject, Being can see Itself torn into the bits and pieces of existence, each part cut off from every other one. Only human beings are able to make the value judgment that the way things are is not the way they ought to be.

Above all, a human can find reason to hope for something better. He can realize that when he ceases to perceive the world, the world will cease to exist for him at least—and that what applies to him in particular applies to all subjects in general. Without a perceiving subject, there can be no perceived object, and without a subject or object there can be no world. If the shade is ever drawn over the last window, the world beyond it will end altogether; with nothing to see, the eye of Being will close, bringing the state of existence to a close. (Please refer to figures 8a through 8d.)

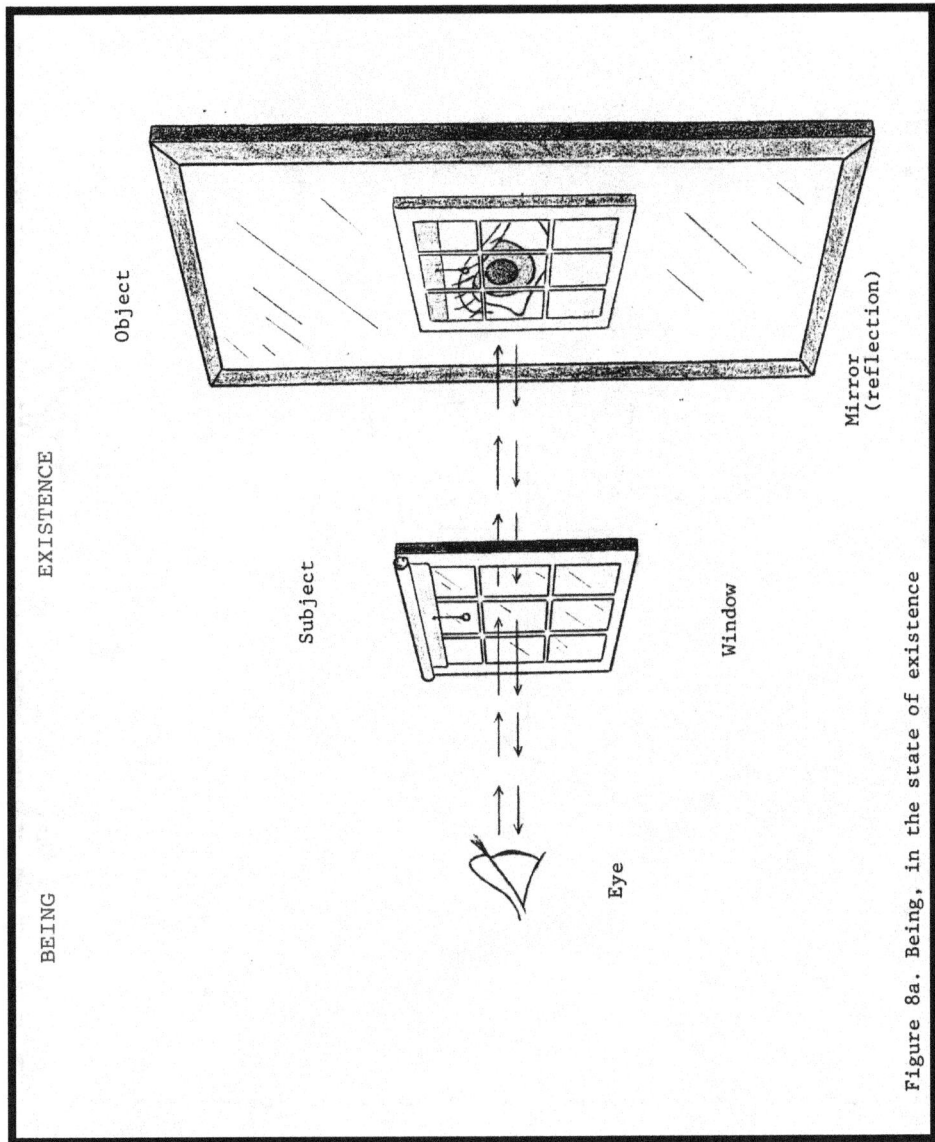

Figure 8a. Being, in the state of existence

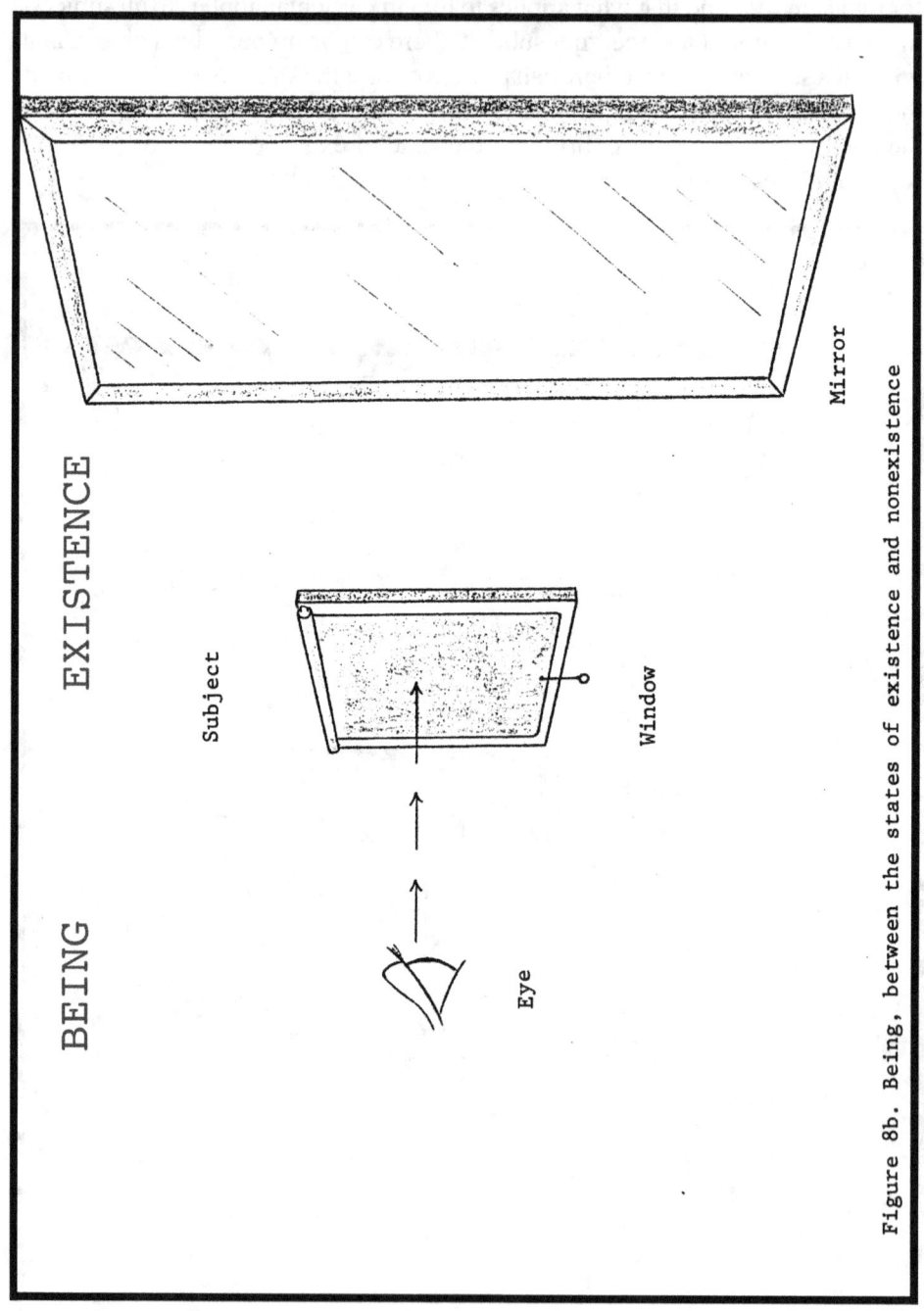

Figure 8b. Being, between the states of existence and nonexistence

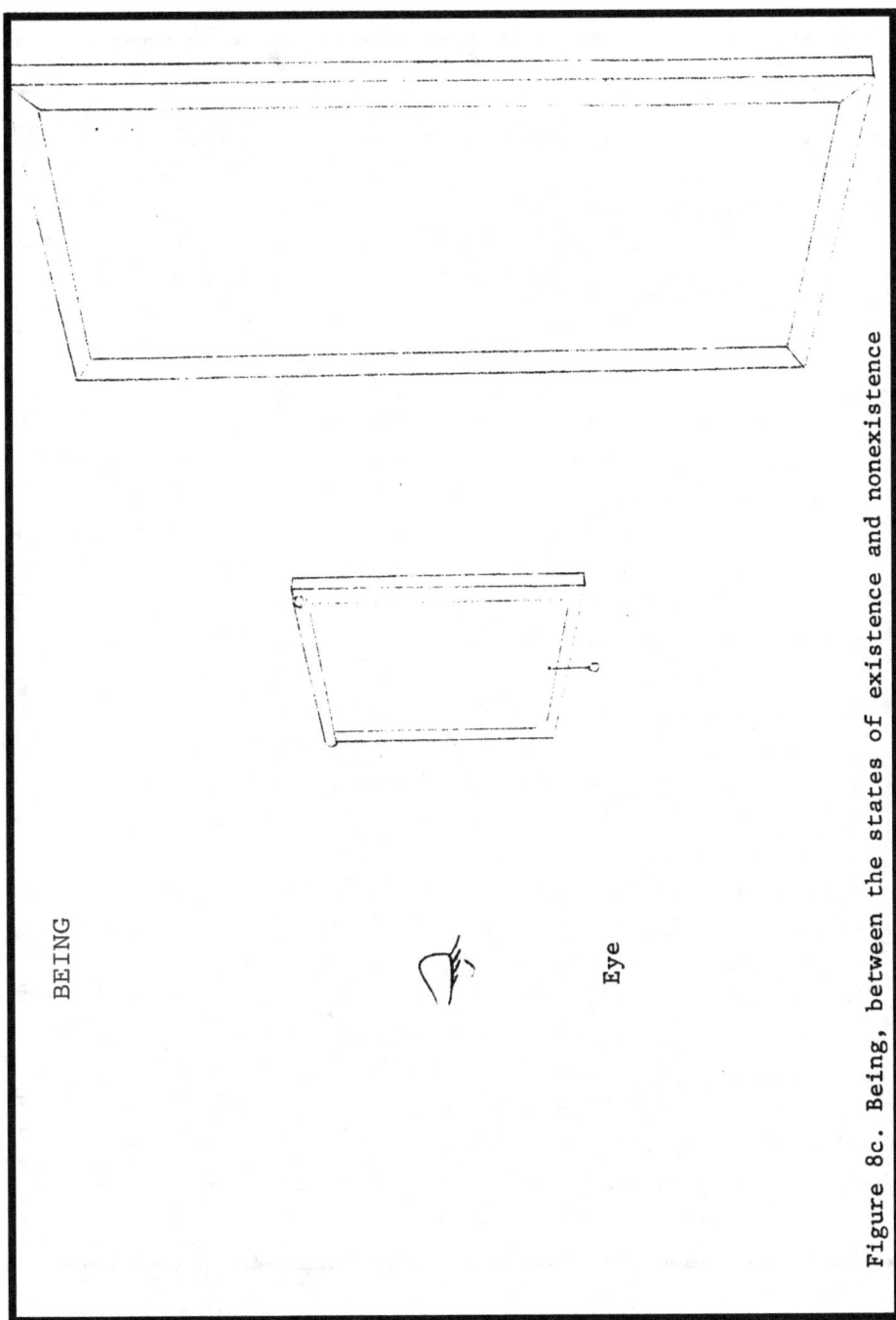

Figure 8c. Being, between the states of existence and nonexistence

Figure 8d. Being, in the state of nonexistence

Q. If a tree falls in the forest where there is no conscious being to hear it, would it make a sound?
A. No.
Q. Would the world continue to exist if there were no conscious being left to perceive it?
A. No—for the same reason.

The end of the world—it's a lot to hope for, but then man has always been good at hoping for what he wants. His desires are so sacred to him that he is willing to endure almost anything in order to satisfy them. He imagines that the things he wants are good, rarely pausing to reflect that they may be good only because he wants them.

All desires are fragments of one desire. The desire for existence and the things that exist is a perverted desire for Being Itself. No matter how many objects they may acquire, subjects are never satisfied. Beings cannot be content with anything less than Being, and that is what they really want.

When a human being is expelled into the world, he is severed from his origin. He is cut off from pure Being and from all other beings. To compensate for his sense of loss, he attempts to control or possess as many other beings as possible. He tries to have what he cannot be. But it's no use, because nothing can ever indemnify him for what he has lost.

Each human being gains the world at a cost to his own soul. To enter the world, he must imprison his soul in a body. ("whilst we are at home in the body, we are absent from the Lord." [II Corinthians 5:7]) The body is made of corruptible matter, while the soul is pure energy. As a subject, each being is locked inside his own body, or person; his personality represents his unique (and therefore limited) perspective on the world.

When the being dies, his body perishes; but his soul goes on forever, since its energy has not been created and can never be destroyed. It is the same energy that quickens every other being alive in the world. There are many bodies, but there is only one soul; many beings, but only One Being. Its unity is the price that Being must pay for existence.

For beings like us, life is existence, but for Being Itself, life is nonexistence—or what we would call "death." Only the state of nonexistence allows Being to be Itself: pure, perfect and completely at One with Itself. The state of existence rends Being asunder, scattering the pieces throughout time and space. Existence brings the world into being and beings into the world. As the precondition of subjectivity, life sustains the world and keeps Being in the state of existence.

Man has made a practice of worshiping false gods. His pursuit of pleasure has brought him pain. He has learned, to his chagrin, that good implies evil. He has sought knowledge by attempting to name, number and measure the countless objects in the world; but, for all that, he has not acquired wisdom. ("Ever learning, but never able to come to the knowledge of the truth." [II Timothy 3:7]) In hallowing power, man has forsaken his freedom. Above all he has worshipped life, even though life is the source of all his problems.

This world isn't big enough for God and man—so God left it. If God gave His life for man on the cross, then only by giving up his life can man resurrect the Supreme Being and thereby restore the state of nonexistence. Then and only then will there be a peace "which passeth all understanding," for there will be nothing more to understand.

Despairing of life while having faith in death offers us profound solace. It leaves us with nothing of value to lose and all to gain. Rather than remaining parts of the world, we can look forward to being at one with God. ("He that loveth his life shall lose it; and he that hateth his life in this world shall keep it unto life eternal." [John 12:25])

God is not only dead. God is death. And, for that reason, He should be worshipped above all else.

Conclusion:
The Problem and the Solution

The world asks no questions, and it gives no answers. It's just there, and it doesn't need a reason to be. If a human being needs a reason to go on living in it, his desires provide more than one reason.

Every desire springs from a lack of some kind. To satisfy his desire, a person tries to obtain what he feels he is lacking. Anything that might thwart his desire he perceives as a problem.

The problems of life are many and complex. We have trouble dealing with the world around us, with our fellow human beings and even with ourselves. There is no end to life's problems because there is no end to our desires. The satisfaction of one desire only gives rise to another; life is one thing after another.

First, we desire to exist. Next we seek the means to existence. If we are able to meet our basic physical needs, we then attempt to satisfy desires that, in this life, can never be completely satisfied. Unsatisfied desires are problems that we have yet to solve.

As we study the various objects in the world to satisfy our desire for knowledge, we discover that existence itself is but the perception of an object (the world or one of its parts) by a subject (a living being, like you, that is conscious of the world or its parts). Existence is one state of Being, in which the One Being becomes many beings as it is reflected (through subjects) in the innumerable objects of the world. The other state of Being is nonexistence, in which Being remains pure, unperceived and at One with Itself.

Our quest for knowledge leads us to perceive as many objects as possible. By labeling, measuring and enumerating things, we strive to assert control over them and the world that they comprise. Because no one subject could possibly perceive (let alone understand) all objects, the thirst for knowledge can never be quenched.

The search for absolute truth is likewise vain. As mere parts of the world, we cannot grasp the whole truth about it. Each of us sees the world from his own limited viewpoint, and all of us believe what we want to believe. In general, we judge a concept to be true insofar as it enables us to live in the world and to adapt thereto—and to adapt the world to ourselves. We may choose to believe what our rulers tell us or what the majority of our peers believe, but, more than anything else, we desire to believe whatever gives us pleasure or relieves our pain.

Pain and pleasure are those qualities of our perceptions that give each subject a vested interest in the world. The subject cannot afford to be indifferent to existence when some parts of it make him feel "good" and others make him feel "bad." Pain is the positive sensation we experience when our bodies encounter resistance from other bodies or when our desires are otherwise frustrated. As the alleviation of pain, pleasure is essentially negative. Because we hate and fear pain, we call it "evil"; conversely, we refer to pleasure as "good" because we love and desire it. We can never feel too much pleasure or too little pain.

What we want and what we get are often two different things, owing to the limitations placed upon us by nature and society. Our bodies are our first limitations, and they define each of us as one object among all the other objects in the world. Making us needy and vulnerable, our bodies throw us at the mercy of both nature and society. We must always obey the laws of nature, but we may violate man-made laws at the risk of being hurt or even destroyed by our rulers.

In any group, someone has to lead and someone else has to follow. Our leaders, with the help of their enforcers, compel obedience by playing upon our desires and fears. If we do as our rulers tell us, then they will permit us to go on pursuing our own happiness within the limits of their law. But if we defy them, they may punish us with fines, imprisonment or execution.

Freedom is risky. If everyone were free to do exactly as he pleased, there's no telling what might happen. By depriving each individual subject of his freedom, the rulers provide society as a whole with the security it requires for long-term, large-scale collective efforts. Most people will not work for each other unless they feel reasonably certain that they will get something in return for their labor—and be able to keep it. They won't invest their time, money or energy in collaborative enterprises without some assurance of a return on their investment. With its power to enforce interpersonal obligations, government furnishes employers and employees alike with the assurances they need. Slaves serve their masters out of necessity.

Man is doomed to live under one form of tyranny or another. Even if he had no human masters, he would remain a slave to passion. His emotions determine what he will do, while his reason simply decides how he can do it. He can exercise only limited control over his environment, in which everything appears to be the effect of a prior cause. Each person's fate results from the interaction of his internal impulses with his external circumstances.

To improve his circumstances, the egoist acquires as many desirable objects as possible, while the altruist helps other people acquire such objects for themselves. Unfortunately, there are always more desiring subjects in the world than there are desirable objects. Furthermore, almost all the raw materials of the world are useless to human beings until human labor transforms them into useful commodities, and so most people need other people to work for them (i.e., to supply them with goods and services) if they are to prosper or even survive.

Government leaders administer economic systems in order to allocate scarce resources among the members of their societies. Though these systems vary in detail, they all draw guidelines for deciding what shall be produced, how much shall be produced and who shall receive the finished products. The rulers always allocate more to themselves than to their subjects, but no one is completely satisfied with what he has. Everybody wants more.

If they cannot get what they want in the socially approved way, some people will try to get it by other means. They will ignore the rules made by their rulers and attempt to make their own rules, by using force if they deem it necessary. Economic discontent spawns crime at home and war abroad.

Even after the shooting stops, life remains a war of each one against all others. It can be nothing else when there are too many people and not enough to go around. Scarcity breeds competition, and competition leads to war.

Everyone perceives himself as both a subject and an object, while perceiving others merely as objects. Because each person can feel only his own desires and fears, his own pleasures and pains, he must rank his own interests above all others. (A conflict of interests is at the bottom of all interpersonal conflicts.) Two or more people join forces only for the purpose of fighting their common enemy.

The world itself is a theater of war. Here subjects oppose objects and vice-versa. Subjects resist each other and objects do the same. One form of life preys upon another, while the brute forces of nature pose constant threats to life in every form. Atoms and molecules must collide with each other just to produce heat and motion. If there were no war, there could be no world.

It would be easy to despair in a world like this—if it weren't for the urgency of our desires. These emotions goad us to continue struggling for existence even if we have no logical reason for doing so. The craving for pleasure and the abhorrence of pain will not be stilled with mere arguments: When we're hungry, we want to eat—whether or not we feel that life is worth the trouble. Our desires, if nothing else, are sacred to us.

Some people feel that their desires require a divine sanction. They need to believe that the things they want are the same ones that a god in heaven wants. In turning to religion, they seek to do God's will and their own at the same time.

That God would want what we want, though, is inconceivable. By definition, the Supreme Being is perfect and therefore Self-sufficient. While we imperfect beings cannot know exactly what the perfect Being is, we can at least have an idea of what It is not, based upon our direct acquaintance with imperfection.

God is not part of the world in which we live, not even the highest part. As the One and Only Being, God cannot be one more being among all the beings that exist in the world. God does not exist at all. He just is—that's All.

God is Being Itself, and the world is existence. In creating the world, God ceases to be—as the perfect, Infinite Being becomes a multitude of imperfect, finite beings, namely, the subjects and objects that make existence possible. (God has no parts, but the world has many.) In Creation, the ideal becomes real and the potential becomes actual. When Being passes from the state of nonexistence to that of existence, It stops being nothing and starts becoming everything, to wit, the things of the world in time and space. Potential energy becomes kinetic; then energy, which is the capacity for change, becomes matter, which is the embodiment of change, as every thing is in flux. (The story of Christ makes a fitting allegory for the destruction of God by the very world that He created.)

But All is not lost. It can never be. There is no place for It to go. Everything comes from Being, and everything can return to It.

Being enters the state of existence because, in Its own way, It desires to—because It can desire only what It lacks, and It lacks only existence. The all-powerful Being can satisfy Its desire without any problem, as It creates existence out of Itself. In religious parlance, God creates the world out of nothing.

The world is all that is left of God. The subjects and objects in it are His remains, since all beings are fragments of the Supreme Being. God is dead, but we, His subjects, can resurrect Him whenever we want.

All we have to do is to stop existing. And, sooner or later, each of us will. It's that simple.

God committed no error when He created the world. He satisfied His one and only desire without any real cost to Himself. True, He ceased to be the One and Only Being when He created the many beings of the world out of Himself, but since Being Itself is essentially nothing, He had nothing to lose and everything (i.e., every thing) to gain. If His creatures suffer, that's their problem—not His. God doesn't have any problems, and He doesn't make any mistakes.

We, however, may be sadly mistaken to cling so doggedly to existence. Life costs us dearly. If we plan to keep paying the high cost of living, we should at least make sure that we get what we pay for.

Regrettably, the cost of life does not always equal its value. Few of us ever receive what we feel to be an adequate return on the time and energy that we invest in life. Yet we go on paying through the nose. Why?

This life is all we know. Regardless of how much we may suffer in the world, we usually prefer to stick with a known evil than to risk exchanging it for an uncertain good. (Better to "bear those ills we have/Than fly to others that we know not of.") We desire life mostly because we fear death.

Maybe we have things backwards. Perhaps we should fear what we now desire and desire what we now fear.

We desire life because we feel that it will bring us pleasure. Our reasoning is correct as far as it goes, for most of us get some pleasure out of life. Pleasure, though, is nothing but the alleviation of pain, and so we have to feel bad before we can feel good. As a matter of fact, life provides us with more than enough opportunities to feel bad.

We fear death because we feel that it will bring us pain, but we are wrong—dead wrong. There is nothing in our experience to indicate that death is painful. (In our fear, we tend to confuse death with dying, which is the last [and often the most painful] part of living.) Death itself is the termination of all pain, since it is the end of all consciousness. As such, it qualifies as the greatest—and the most lasting—of all pleasures and, thus, the highest conceivable good.

Even if the desire for existence is instinctive, it is not uncontrollable for that reason. The mark of a civilized person is his ability to subdue his instincts. Accordingly, civilization could score its highest achievement by conquering the lowest and most basic instinct of all—the instinct for self-preservation. Unlike other animals, a human being can renounce his will to live.

Not that life is a total loss. It can always serve as a learning experience. In the school of hard knocks that he calls the world, man can learn the invaluable lesson that life is not worth living. In his struggle for existence, he can come to realize that existence isn't worth the struggle.

While Being is Absolute Truth, existence is the knowledge of relative truths. If we could just go beyond the jumble of names and numbers that passes for knowledge, we might discover the only four truths worth knowing:

1. Life is pain.
2. Pain arises from desire and fear.
3. The way to end pain is to end desire and fear.
4. The way to end desire and fear is to end life.

These, the Four Ignoble Truths of Life, are as dismal as they are undeniable. But the truth is the truth—even when it hurts.

Surely it does not comfort us to think that life is a fate worse than death, yet that is exactly what it is for the vast majority of human beings. The pain that they suffer by far exceeds the pleasure they enjoy. Their lives are heavy burdens that they shoulder with great difficulty.

It takes a special kind of person to love life, one who accepts it for what it is—a problem-solving activity. Such a person lives life as if he were playing a game, and plays it avidly by the rules laid down by nature and/or society, being gratified by victory and inspired by defeat to play with even greater zeal. The lover of life views every problem as an opportunity, a challenge to which he can respond creatively. Whether or not he wins first prize, he plays the game for its own sake and keeps on playing until it is all over.

Most of us love life in the beginning; but from the moment at which we start to take it seriously, life changes from a pleasant game into a "serious" business. Play turns to work, as obligation supersedes inclination. No longer are we supposed to do things because we want to—but instead because we have to. We learn to accept "responsibility," meaning that we grow accustomed to serving others. (An "irresponsible" person is one who tries to satisfy his own desires instead of other people's desires.)

The only thing in the world that we really have to take seriously is pain. Its persuasive immediacy cannot be ignored. ("For there was never yet philosopher/That could endure the toothache patiently.") Anyone who can laugh off his own pain is a superman, and anyone who can laugh off the pain of others is a monster.

Our rulers use pain to teach us responsibility, that is, to force us to do what they want. Our parents may spank us or send us to bed without supper. Our teachers may keep us after school or banish us to the principal's office. Our commanding officers may throw us in the brig or court-martial us. Our bosses may dock or fire us. The police can arrest, beat or shoot us. Judges can impose fines or sentence us to prison or death. And even if we manage to escape punishment in this world, we won't be so lucky in the next one—where God will fry our fannies forever. Not even death, then, can furnish us with a refuge from our rulers, or so they say.

If we choose to believe them, then we become their complaisant slaves. We will render them lifelong service as their workers, consumers, enforcers and worshippers. Because of the club they hold over us, we must continue to obey them as long as we fear pain and death.

An eagerness to avoid pain is understandable, but our fear of death is hard to fathom. There is no valid reason to assume that death itself is the least bit painful. Fear of the unknown cannot be cited to justify the fear of death, for we know exactly what happens to the deceased: He stops performing physiological functions such as those connected with the nervous system, whose operation is indispensable for the perception of pain and pleasure and everything else.

For the dead, everything ceases to exist. They perceive nothing because they lack the means to perception. The dead are incapable of being seduced or bullied by the world. (Lucky stiffs!)

Not so the living. Our sentient bodies place us in the power of nature and society. Unless we actually enjoy solving all the problems that life poses, we cannot help but feel that life is the only real problem and that death is the only permanent solution to it.

Even if we could feed, clothe, shelter and educate everyone; even if we could do away with unemployment, poverty, pollution, injustice, crime, war, disease and death itself; even then the main problem would still be with us. Life is the be-all of problems, and death is the end-all.

That's right. Death is the cure-all.

Just think of how great it was not to be alive! You had no desires to satisfy, no fears to allay and no problems to solve. All your troubles began on the day you were born, and they will not end until the day you die.

Only death can solve our problems once and for all. Everything else is merely a stopgap. Knowledge of arbitrary names and numbers allows us to exert some control over the world, but, for the most part, the world still controls us. The enjoyment of earthly pleasures presupposes the suffering of earthly pains. As commonly displayed, love is not the answer, for it usually involves a selfish desire for possession and can easily turn to hatred when that desire is thwarted. The desire for freedom is always thwarted in a world bound by civic and cosmic necessity. The economic system of every society is rigged in favor of its rulers, but that's the only way that it can be: It's their system, after all. The struggle for wealth, power and even mere survival makes life a war of each person against all others, in which peace is an illusion. Putting our faith in human beings (even when they claim to speak for God) leads inevitably to despair—when we find out that those human beings are only human.

Death is the logical conclusion to be drawn from the premises of life. Life's major premise is that whatever has a beginning must also have an end.

In more ways than one is death the end of life. It is life's goal as well as its conclusion. ("The aim of all life is death.") And if death is the end, then life is the means to it.

Death is all around us. For all we know, our Earth may be hurtling through a dead universe. Even if there is life on other planets, it must be extremely rare. Life is the exception, not the rule.

In all probability, life began by accident. Activated by energy, a few particles of matter combined to produce the first living thing. The odds were against life from the beginning, as the first live being was probably crushed by the dead beings all around it. But the desire for existence was strong enough to impel other life forms produced over millions of years to survive and spread throughout the Earth. As life evolved from simple microbes into complex organisms, its capacity for consciousness rose until it reached its zenith in man.

Of all animals, man perceives the world most clearly. His senses may not be as keen as those of other animals, but he is superior in his ability to reflect upon his sensations and thereby form concepts and make value judgments. Man alone is aware of his own death.

Other animals aren't afraid of death. They don't even know what it is. Doing what comes naturally to them, they simply respond to their bodies' affinity for pleasure and aversion to pain.

Small children don't fear death either. They are taught to fear it. Their elders fill their poor little heads with threats and horror stories about death. ("Life is good and death is bad ... very, very bad." "If you die, you won't be able to play with your toys or watch TV anymore." "Be careful! Do you want to get killed?" "Do what I say or I'll kill you!")

By adulthood, most people are scared to death of death. Their society has conditioned them to believe that death is the worst of all possible evils. People are prepared to do almost anything their rulers tell them in order to avoid it.

A moment's thought, however, could undo a lifetime of brainwashing. Life, not death, is the source of all our problems. No sooner have we solved one problem than another takes its place. And our problems will not end until we do.

There is no use in trying to increase the quantity or to improve the quality of life, for life is irredeemable. ("You can't make a silk purse out of a sow's ear.") Things can be no better than they are. New solutions to old problems only breed new problems. (A life without problems is like a square without corners—it doesn't exist.) The world can be reformed, but it can never be remade. Its outward form may change, but its substance remains the same.

All attempts to remake society, whether peaceful or violent, are doomed to failure. Government is the means employed by the rulers to exploit their subjects, and its function will not change—no matter who's in charge. Utopia can never be built on the cracked foundation of human nature.

The powerful can be defeated only through the loss of their power base. Rulers need subjects, and the subjects keep providing their rulers with fresh supplies of workers, consumers and enforcers. Without new slaves, the masters would soon have to hang up their whips.

Human labor is the source of all wealth and power. The few people on top need many on the bottom to do the dirty and dangerous work for them. Winners would be lost without losers.

The people who have to fight the wars never win them. On the contrary, they stand to lose everything that they have. Only those who stay safely behind the lines can win—no matter which side they're on. But whether the battles are fought between individuals or groups, war is one of the coldest, hardest facts of life, while peace is a pleasant fiction suitable solely for dreams or sermons. The only way to stop making war is to stop making warriors.

The only real peace of mind is a total absence of mind. A mind can never be at peace. When our problems don't besiege us all at once, they harass us one at a time. Disaster may threaten at every turn, but if we don't have big troubles, then we worry about little things. If we could have everything we ever wanted, we would be afraid of losing it (and someday we would have to lose it). One way or another, we will have something to worry about as long as we live.

After we die, we will have no more yesterdays to regret, no more todays to endure and no more tomorrows to dread. There will be nothing more for us to worry about because we will have nothing left to worry with. Our consciousness will expire, leaving the world with no further opportunities to assail us. For the dead, the world does not exist. All pain is in the brain, and so the pain dies when the brain does.

When we're dead, we don't have to do anything. In life we must attend to a host of unpleasant necessities. Nature and society are hard taskmasters.

With their innumerable laws and penalties, my rulers can force me to act in almost any way they like. They can discourage me from robbing, assaulting or murdering my neighbor. They can oblige me to respect his legal rights and even to support him in his poverty, disability and old age. But they cannot make me love him.

No power on Earth—or in Heaven—can make me love my neighbor merely by ordering me to do so and threatening to penalize me if I don't. I can't even make myself do that. For I have no more control over my feelings than I have over the beating of my own heart. (Of course, the all-powerful God could easily change the way I think and feel about everything if He wanted to—but apparently He doesn't.) I will love another person only to the extent that he satisfies my desires; otherwise, I will hate and fear that person as long as I look upon him as something separate and apart from me, as one more object confronting me in a hostile world.

Before I can truly love my neighbor, I must view him as a subject like myself—not just as the object of my desire or fear. I have to feel that he has his own desires and fears and that he can be pleased or pained by the objects of his perception. Through no fault of my own, though, I have trouble doing this.

Each person has been sentenced to solitary confinement inside his own body. As the prisoner of his individual consciousness, he is on the inside looking out. The subject can perceive nothing but his own perceptions. As long as he lives, he can never go beyond himself. Even if he manages to think of something beside himself, it is still his self that does the thinking. The self and the other can never be reconciled in this life.

In the state of existence, everything makes a difference; in the state of nonexistence, nothing does. Every thing in this world is different from every other thing, as each subject distinguishes between itself and the various objects of its perception. Out of this world, in the realm of pure Being, there is nothing. No beings to perceive or to be perceived and, thus, no distinctions to be made between the self and the other, between mine and thine. There, All is One.

While we exist, we are part of a world whose parts cannot help but run afoul of each another. For the world to have peace, all the beings in it would have to function as one being. But the interaction of their internal impulses with their external circumstances makes such universal harmony impossible. Driven by his own desires, each person seeks his own ends and regards other people as the means to those ends or as enemies. He will unite with other people only for the sake of fighting a mutual foe. The upshot is war.

It takes more than one being to make war, and there are more than enough beings in the world to ensure perpetual conflict. In the state of nonexistence, however, there are no more beings at all. There is no more than One Being, the One Being from which all beings emerge. In this, the cradle of Being, there is but One Self, Being Itself, and no other with which It could possibly clash. The state of nonexistence is truly a peace which passeth all understanding. And a peace to be desired.

The world resembles a jigsaw puzzle whose parts fit together imperfectly. Trying to force them together only produces friction and causes abrasion. All of us exist as pieces of the world, torn apart by impulse and circumstance. In the seamless whole of Being, we will be One. Gone will be the desires and fears that now pit each one of us against all the others. The pieces cannot help falling together.

Existence entails limitations, namely, the spatiotemporal boundaries that divide one thing from another in the world. To exist is to stand out from Being and from every other being. Each being can stand out from Being for only so long before falling back into It. Being is the ground of all beings, the source of their existence. Eventually, every single one must fall to the ground and return to its source. Every thing with a beginning must also have an ending.

Nonexistence knows no bounds. Neither nature nor society can impose limits upon the Infinite Being. It has no beginning or ending in space and time.

Everything that exists lacks something, and from the perception of this lack spring the desires and fears that drive conscious beings to seek pleasure and to avoid pain. Pure Being does not exist; It is nothing. The One and Only cannot be helped or hurt by anything because—in the state of nonexistence—there is nothing besides Being.

Being Itself is nothing, that is, no existing thing. Each being is something, that is, some existing thing. Each being comes from Being Itself.

Q. How can something come from nothing?
A. Only through perception.

Existence is nothing but the perception of one thing (an object) by another thing (a subject). Without a subject to perceive it, no being could exist as an object. It might still be, but it could not stand out from the ground of Being or from other beings. If a being could not perceive itself and/or other beings, it could not exist as a subject. Unless a being can perceive or be perceived, it cannot exist at all.

Perception, by its very nature, is potentially painful. Subject and object exist in opposition to one another, and the subject suffers when this opposition grows too intense for it. No matter how stoical a subject may be, there is always an object that can harm it. (Mortals always live in mortal danger.)

Why people are willing to put up with so many problems just for the sake of living is hard to comprehend—but not impossible. If he does not overlook his immortal soul completely, the average person tends to confuse it with his mortal personality. The personality is just one form taken in matter by the soul.

Energy materializes as a body, or person, and all the physical (and thus mental) qualities of the person make up his personality.

The personality dies with the person, as the body ceases to function and loses its form, but the energy that formed and animated that person goes on forever with the capacity to embody itself in other material forms. The energy of Being is the soul of the universe. There are many bodies, but there is only one soul. There are many beings, but there is only One Being.

All temporal beings come from the eternal Being. Sensing its kinship with the immortal, each conscious being feels that it will live forever. Nonhuman beings don't even know about death, while the human ones try their best to forget about it. ("Have you ever thought, as a hearse rolled by, that one day you are going to die?")

We live under an illusion of immortality. Although we may accept the inevitability of death on an intellectual level, we reject it on an emotional one. By the time our time comes, we tell ourselves, medical science may have discovered a cure for whatever might ail us. And even if we must die, we won't have to do so until tomorrow—and tomorrow never comes: The past is dead and the future is yet to be born. The present is truly alive, and so are we. Should tomorrow actually arrive, we can still look forward to the day after tomorrow, when we hope to begin an afterlife of endless todays.

If we knew when we were going to die—right down to the last second—then few of us would act or think in the same way that we do now. We would probably spend far less time and energy working to acquire things, because we would know the exact moment at which we were going to lose them all. We could appreciate that the struggle for existence is futile, as the clock on the wall would be constantly reminding us that, no matter how hard we strive to survive, we will die by and by. Above all, we would be able to see that in the end nothing really matters.

Life is a joke. We may not feel like laughing when the joke's on us and the punch line's a killer, but—if we have any sense of humor at all—we have to admit that our basic situation is comical. Everything that we might gain in the beginning or the middle of life will surely be lost in the end. (In the end, we're all losers.) And for all the pains that we take to stay alive, we will soon be dead. It's all for nothing—because it's all from nothing.

Being Itself is nothing. It is no thing that perceives or is perceived by anything else, for (in the state of nonexistence) there is nothing other than Being. Although pure Being does not exist, It is the ground and source of all existence. Everything comes from nothing.

Existence is all that nonexistent Being lacks, and so existence is all that It can desire. As the all-powerful Being, It can satisfy Its desire for existence without any difficulty, creating the world out of Its own nothingness. When It enters the state of existence, the One Being becomes many beings; pure energy changes into corruptible matter; consciousness arises from the unconscious; time begins; space expands; and God turns into animal, mineral, vegetable and everything else in the world. Where there was nothing anywhere, there is now something everywhere.

In passing from the state of nonexistence to that of existence, the whole of Being divides Itself into the parts of the world. Some of these parts (the objects) can hurt the other parts (the subjects). Pain is the price of perception.

The world was not created at any one point in time, for the world is not in time. Instead, time is in the world—as time, like space, is merely a way in which the parts of the world relate to each other. Creation is an ongoing process. Every moment is a new beginning.

Being Itself began the world by bringing Itself to an end. In Its stead appeared a multitude of beings, the subjects and objects without which existence would be impossible. Being, in effect, created the world by destroying Itself.

Each subject creates a part of the world by perceiving it. The whole world would amount to the sum total of its subjects' perceptions—if there were someone or something capable of summing up those perceptions. But there isn't. From any point in space, only one subject at a time can view the world. The world, therefore, exists only in bits and pieces.

The world was and is created piece by piece, and it is uncreated in the same way. Being Itself perceives nothing because—in the state of nonexistence—there is nothing other than Being. In the state of existence, there is nothing besides beings, and only subjective beings can perceive the objects of the world. The birth of each subject is the beginning of a part of the world, and the death of that subject is the end of that part.

Q. Will the world ever end?
A. It will for you.

Sooner or later, the world will end for you and me and everyone else. We are just parts of the world, but the world is nothing but its parts. The world needs us—or creatures like us—to keep it going.

Existence is perception, which requires subjects and objects. Without a subject, there can be no object, and without subjects like you and me, the world would vanish without a trace. The world, in part, is our creation.

The priests say that only God has the power of life and death. Maybe they're right. Yet it's the easiest thing in the world for one person to destroy a life—and the second easiest for two people to create one.

Apparently, God has delegated the power of life and death to us. Being Itself has given human beings the choice between existence and nonexistence. Death is the door to nonexistence.

Q. Why are we here?
A. Because we desire to be here, or fear not to be.

We exist because we desire existence or fear nonexistence. All conscious beings do the same. Unconscious beings exist because there are conscious beings alive to perceive them. The world will not end altogether as long as there is one subject left to perceive it. Life is the prerequisite of existence.

To be or not to be is not the question. Where Being is concerned, we have no choice whatsoever. Being will always be, though existence need not always exist. Either Being will be Itself (in Its state of nonexistence) or the world of beings (in its state of existence).

Q. To exist or not to exist? That is the question.
A. Not to exist. That is the answer.

For every problem, there is at least one solution. Death alone can relieve all our pain and put all our desires and fears to rest forever. It is the only panacea.

Only death can bring us to the state of nonexistence, where All is One. No longer will we be many beings at war with each other. We will be freed from the bodies and minds that are the sources of so much torment to us. Death, indeed, is the great liberator.

Being Itself is free to exist or not to exist—and so is a human being. Once Being has satisfied Its own desire for existence, the beings of the world fall under the rule of natural and/or human laws, but humans may cast off their yokes whenever they choose. Life goes on, only because we want it to.

Each person is drafted into the human race. No one has the option of enlisting in it. If all of us, in fact, could have known beforehand precisely how our lives were going to turn out, many of us might have asked not to be born.

After the cursed events have taken place, however, it is too late for us to second-guess our parents. We're already here, and there are only three things we can do about it. We can struggle for existence or give up the struggle or end our existence outright. Most of us opt to struggle.

At the dawn of life, our desire for existence is reflexive. We cling, suck and cry for our very lives. Although unaware of our own mortality at that tender age, we instinctively preserve ourselves by seeking pleasure and avoiding pain (just like the other animals).

By the time we are old enough to make rational decisions, living has become a habit. So accustomed have we grown to breathing that we can hardly imagine what it would be like never to draw another breath. The persistent stimuli of pleasure and pain have addicted us to our own existence. We're hooked, and it's very hard for us to just say "no" to life.

That the habit should be so hard to kick is understandable. Life has only one entrance but many exits, and few of the latter are very appealing. Death is the door to nonexistence, but pain usually stands guard at the doorway. It is not the least bit self-contradictory to desire death but to fear dying.

But not to worry, help is on the way. Death will cure us of our addiction to life and everything that goes with it.

Benjamin Franklin said that the only sure things in life are death and taxes. He was half right. If you're poor enough—or rich enough—then you won't have to pay any taxes at all; but, rich or poor, everyone must die. Death represents the only security attainable by humankind. It is the one thing in this world that we can count on.

When we aren't working to preserve our lives, we're doing everything possible to escape from them. Athletes, entertainers, novelists, pushers and bartenders can pocket so much of our cash because they enable us to flee from the misery or the tedium of our lives—but just for the moment. Only death provides us with a permanent escape. It permits us to make a clean getaway from the world.

Some lives are less miserable than others. Thanks to death, though, every life has a happy ending. Many people grumble about living and dying, but no one has ever lodged a complaint against death based on his own experience of it. ("Don't knock it till you've tried it!") The cure-all has no unpleasant side effects that anyone alive knows of. And, if we want to be rational, then we should predicate our opinions on the things we know.

The best thing about the cure-all is that it works automatically. No one has to go to his death, because death comes to everyone. Suicide is unnecessary.

Even though we may never be able to renounce our desire for existence, the world will eventually end our ability to exist. If society doesn't kill us, then nature will. One way or the other, our lives will end and so will our problems.

Death wipes our slates clean. When we're dead, it won't matter whether we were skinny or fat, rich or poor, happy or unhappy, innocent or guilty. And our deaths will last a lot longer than our lives did.

> Fear not the sentence of death,
>> remember them that have been before thee, and that come after;
>> for this is the sentence of the Lord over all flesh.
> And why art thou against the pleasure of the most High?
>> there is no inquisition in the grave,
>> whether thou have lived ten, or an hundred, or a thousand years.
>>> (Ecclesiasticus 41:3-4,
>>>> from the 1769 Oxford King James Bible,
>>>> authorized version)

All of us will be saved. We came from nothing, and we will return to nothing. After we die, it is finished—unless we have started something new.

To end it all, all we have to do is stop beginning it again. The human race, which has existed for tens of thousands of years, would vanish in little more than one century were it not renewed periodically. The propagation of the species—and with it the perpetuation of human suffering—will continue only as long we allow it to. Our extinction would be no loss to the world, since we humans have accomplished precious little on Earth beyond polluting the environment, depleting natural resources, fostering injustice and slaughtering millions of living beings (including those of our own kind). The only thing that our race is really good at is breeding—too good, in fact, with seven billion people crowding the planet and creating more problems than we could hope to solve in a trillion lifetimes.

Our bodies serve as disposable containers for DNA. Our body cells die with our bodies, but our germ cells are potentially immortal, as the gametes from two different individuals join to produce a new individual. (Old chromosomes never die—they just replicate.)

Every birth is a tragedy waiting to unfold. No one can foresee what will happen to an infant after he is pulled into a world as unpredictable as ours. ("On the day you were born, you were old enough to die.") If he is not cut down at birth, will the child grow into a culprit ... or a victim ... or both? The odds are that he will both inflict and endure an immeasurable amount of pain before suffering his final throes. Consumed by their own desires, most prospective parents fail to take such matters into consideration.

True love is not a selfish desire for possession. The one who loves truly desires what is best for his beloved, and so the person who truly loves children will not have any of his own. He would not wish to expose his offspring to the same risks and hardships he has known in his own life. A loving, caring person knows that the best thing that can be done for generations unborn is to leave them that way.

That way, the sins of the fathers would no longer be visited upon their children or their children's children. No future generations would have to cope with problems bequeathed to them by the present one. They would be free. The cure-all is simple. And for that reason, people who imagine that solutions have to be as complicated as the problems that their forebears have created might reject it.

The living tend to be biased in favor of life. To most of them, the very suggestion that death is a cure-all would seem nothing short of insanity. They may be correct—but, at the same time, madness may be the only rational response to an irrational world.

Everything else has failed. Despite the best efforts of the best people, the world is a mess. Saints and geniuses have tried to save the world, but it's still as lost as it ever was. Death is our last hope ... and the only one that won't let us down.

We're all in the same boat—the Titanic—and sinking fast. But we will find no peace as long as we crowd the lifeboats and hang on to our life preservers. The only way to save ourselves is to give up and let go. Salvation and survival are not synonymous.

The world may have begun with a bang, but it doesn't have to end that way. We don't need an Armageddon to put a period to our misery. The true savior will bring peace on Earth, not a sword.

Death will save us. It will break the grip that we have on the world and that the world has on us. And as long as we have refrained from reproducing ourselves, no one else will have to suffer on our account.

Saving ourselves means losing the world. When each individual dies, our piecemeal world loses a piece of itself; if that piece has not multiplied, then the world's loss is irrecoverable. Death without reproduction is like subtraction without addition: If the process goes on long enough, nothing will be left.

Christians are taught to imitate Christ. Christ was childless; and so, if all of them followed his example, there would soon be no Christians left. Few of us, of course, possess the virtue of a Jesus Christ—but none of us needs to.

We need not be celibate to be sterile. Medical technology provides us with the means to have sex without conception. Nature baits its reproductive trap with a morsel of pleasure; but, as cunning animals, we can steal the bait without ensnaring ourselves or others. Science has given us the power to cheat nature.

All that each part of the world can do is its own part. ("For every man shall bear his own burden." [Galatians 6:5]) When a single human being dies without issue, his part of the world is over and done with. A parent, on the other hand, renews the world by handing down his existence to his offspring. The problems of the parent end at death, but his newborn's problems are just beginning.

The parent has already chosen existence for his child, but now the child must choose for itself. At first the choice is instinctive, as the child's bodily mechanisms push it toward life and away from death. There comes a time, though, when the maturing human is able to look beyond his immediate sensations and to realize that pain is part and parcel of life. It is then that he must ask whether the pleasures of life are worth the pains. In short, whether life is worth living. If he answers in the affirmative, then he will embrace existence and not pass up the chance to pass it on to his progeny. Even if he decides that life is not worth living, his fear of dying may deter him from ending his own life—but it should also discourage him from beginning a new one. The person who accepts life seeks to perpetuate it, while the person who despises it refuses to become one more link in an endless chain.

Anyone who desires life deserves it—and everything that goes with it. (That my sound harsh, but a problem must be faced squarely before it can be solved.)

If the lover of life has ever read a newspaper or a history book or has just taken a good look around, he knows about the natural and man-made disasters that can befall him in this world. Unless he is foolish or stupid, he realizes that bad things don't always happen to other people. He takes a deliberate risk when he chooses existence; so whatever happens, he has it coming.

The same cannot be said of his children. They are his effects, and he is their cause. Thanks to him (and/or his mate), they will have many needs to satisfy and vexations to bear. At the very least, they will have to go places, meet people and do things they would sooner avoid. The worst that could happen is better imagined than described; the point is that anything can happen to them once their progenitors have brought them into the world. Parents always take big chances with their children's lives.

Without protection, sexual intercourse can lead to AIDS, venereal disease or pregnancy. Of the three possible outcomes, pregnancy normally produces the longest illness (viz., life) with the most complications. Death cures all ills, while birth control prevents them altogether.

> ...To die, to sleep–
> No more; and by a sleep to say we end
> The heartache and the thousand natural shocks that flesh is heir to.
> 'Tis a consummation
> Devoutly to be wished. To die, to sleep,
> To sleep—perchance to dream. Aye, there's the rub!
>
> (*Hamlet*, Act III, Scene i)

Q. "For in that sleep of death what dreams may come when we have shuffled off this mortal coil...[?]"
A. We'll find out.

We can decide to believe our rulers when they tell us of the nightmares that await us beyond the veil, in which case we will continue to live and serve them as long as possible. Our fear of annihilation may even prompt us to reproduce ourselves, thus imposing the burden of our own existence on an innocent posterity. We can believe whatever we like; we can have faith in anything we choose. But we're just kidding ourselves if we think that we, or anyone else, can know the unknowable.

We can live in only one world at a time. We already have enough problems in this world without worrying about any that we might encounter in another one. For that matter, there is no reason in this world to believe that there is another one, except in our dreams.

When we dream, our eyes are usually closed—but our mind's eye stays open. Dreams are perceptions like any others, and death ends all perceptions.

Death closes the mind's eye. Consequently, we shouldn't lose any sleep worrying that we might have bad dreams when we've shuffled off our coils.

Life, rather than death, is the province of dreams. ("All that we see or seem/ Is but a dream within a dream.") The sensations we perceive in our sleep are every bit as real as the ones we experience in the course of our waking lives. The difference is that, when we see or hear other people in our dreams, they do not see or hear us as they would in "real" life—or as we assume they would.

None of us can get inside another person's head to perceive what he is perceiving: All the sights and sounds of the world are in our own heads. Each person, in effect, lives inside his own part of the world, and death will bring that part to an end. In the meantime, we will have faith that the world is real when we are awake, just as we have faith that our dreams are real when we are asleep.

If we can have faith in something as uncertain as life, we should have no trouble at all believing in a sure thing like death. Based on our own observations of the dead, we know just what to expect from death. Our bodies, our nervous systems, and thus our minds and sensory apparatuses will cease to function; we will lose the ability to think and feel and dream, period. Anyone with evidence to the contrary should put up or shut up.

After death extinguishes our subjectivity, we no longer exist. We cease to perceive and to be perceived. The corpses we leave behind are no longer our bodies—just empty shells that nature will transform into other objects to be perceived by other subjects.

Death transforms us from something into nothing. In death, we return to that from which we came. At one with Being once again, we are truly home.

Q. If Being Itself spoke to us, what would It say?
A. "I've been nothing, and I've been something. And believe me, nothing is better!"

Being nothing, Being Itself lacks everything and therefore desires existence. To satisfy Its desire, It creates the world of beings out of Itself. Each being reflects Being, however dimly, and so the desire of Being for existence becomes the desire of each conscious being (i.e., each subject), which in turn desires other beings (objects) in order to sustain and enrich its own existence. Because there are more desiring subjects than there are desirable objects, life becomes a war of the former for the latter. This war is unwinnable, since no subject can get everything it wants. Due to the nothingness at the core of its being (a legacy from Being Itself), a subject can never fill the emptiness it feels within itself.

In all innocence did Being create the world. It never meant to harm anyone or anything, let alone Itself. Pure Being had no knowledge of good or evil or anything else.

Not until Being entered the state of existence did It have any way of knowing whether Its world would be good, bad or indifferent. Knowledge is existence, or the perception of an object by a subject. Being Itself perceives nothing and therefore knows nothing, whereas subjects know the objects that they perceive. Being is all-knowing only in the sense that all knowing subjects are ultimately Its beings—and so their knowledge is Its knowledge.

Human beings know what it is to suffer. As the most complex beings on Earth, they have the greatest capacity for both suffering and judgment. From their experience of pleasure and pain, they can derive the concepts of good and evil and then decide whether the good of life justifies the evil, whether the pleasure compensates for the pain. In sum, whether life is worthwhile.

Being Itself is in no position to judge. Nothing can oppose the eternal, Infinite Being in space, and It has no form that will change in time. Yet It is the unlimited potential for change and is, in that sense, all-powerful. It is all-good insofar as all good comes from it, but then so does all evil. Itself nothing, Being is the origin of everything.

> I am the Lord, and there is none else.
> I form the light, and create darkness:
> I make peace, and create evil:
> I the Lord do all these things.
> (Isaiah 45:6-7)

Being has not been Itself lately. It has been something else—the world—ever since Its desire for existence spawned the first subject that perceived its first object. The desire for existence of that subject (or a similar one) caused it to generate a new subject whose own desire led to further reproduction—and so on to the present day. Being created the world, and conscious beings recreate it. Beings reproduce what Being has produced, multiplying one problem by infinity.

The desire of Being for existence set off a continuing chain reaction in which each being forms a link in the existential chain. Each being will come to an end, but existence itself will not end until the last conscious being does. The world will endure as long as conscious beings want it to.

Human beings can call a halt to their existence. Alone among beings, humans possess the knowledge and the power to choose between existence and nonexistence. They alone have the ability to disown their desires.

Unlike Being Itself, human beings are worldly-wise. Whereas Being created the world blindly, conscious beings like ourselves can see what the world is really like. Being had only the potential for suffering, but we know the actuality of pain. We are the ones who live in the world and have to pay the high cost of living, so we are in a position to decide if life is worth all the trouble.

Through our eyes, Being can see the truth. In fact, It can see a different truth through the eyes of each human being, for each of us perceives—and therefore is—a different part of the world. The world is nothing but beings, which are the parts of Being in the state of existence.

Through existence, Being becomes aware of Itself. It discovers, by means of perception, that It is now a thing of shreds and patches, ripped apart and dragged down into the world by the force of Its own desire. Seeing Itself reflected in every being, It can recall longingly what It once was, perfection Itself, the One and Only Being without hope or fear—and without the need for either.

Perfection needs nothing but Itself. God doesn't need the world. ("But when that which is perfect is come,/then that which is in part will be done away." [I Corinthians 13:10]) Existence is superfluous. God is enough, and, through mankind, God becomes aware of Himself.

In Its desire for existence, Being, uncreating Itself, created the world. The Supreme Being died so that lowly beings could live. Man, the highest of the lowly, is the one being capable of understanding both the problem and its built-in solution. He is able to realize that, in one way or another, he will suffer as long as he lives and that his suffering will end after he dies. (At least he can look forward to being dead happily ever after, even if he can't live that way.)

This world isn't big enough for Being Itself and existence too. It is big enough only for existence. Man can have existence, or Being Itself can have nonexistence; there is no third alternative.

The trouble began when Being desired beings, and it will not end until beings desire Being. When Being desired existence, It had nothing to fear from Itself. Beings, however, have good reason to fear other beings. They learn just how hard life can be, and their knowledge becomes Being's knowledge.

Without prior experience of the world, Being committed no error or sin by entering the state of existence. Being nothing, It had nothing to lose and everything in the world to gain; but beings have little to gain and everything to lose in the world, and they would be making a big mistake to go on losing from one generation to the next.

They need not fear that, by despising Creation, they would be committing a sin against the Supreme Being. On the contrary, to reject existence is to accept Being Itself and to reject Its Self-estrangement. In the world, Being is alienated from Itself. It is divided into beings, each one of which is separated from all the others and thereby placed in fundamental opposition to them.

Being Itself is a prisoner of each being. The nothingness that a conscious being feels inside itself, the emptiness that it can never fill, is nothing other than the divine essence of Being, yearning for release from Its earthly confinement. ("The kingdom of God cometh not with observation: Neither shall they say, Lo here! Or, lo, there! For, behold, the kingdom of God is within you." [Luke 17:20-21]) Like a spider caught in its own web, Being struggles to be free.

It desires to be free from fear. Beings were created out of pure desire, but in the world they learned about fear, desire's dark underside. (Anything can happen to a being in the world.) Human beings cannot truly love the world or attribute its creation to a loving God as long as they have something to fear from it—and they have, until death liberates them from it. ("There is no fear in love; but perfect love casteth out fear: because fear hath torment. He that feareth is not made perfect in love." [1 John 4:18])

Pure Being desired existence, whereupon conscious beings were born. That's all there was to it. God didn't know what He was doing when He created the world.

Human beings, on the other hand, cannot plead ignorance as their excuse for perpetuating their existence. They have eaten from the tree of knowledge and tasted the fruit of good and evil. Enlightened by their own experience of life, they know just how bad things can be in the world, yet they choose to bring more beings like themselves into it. How come?

Fear of death or at least of dying can explain why individuals seek to preserve their own lives—but not why they feel a need to reproduce them. A parent's desire for status, comfort in his old age, free farm labor or someone to carry on the family name would hardly seem a sufficient reason for dragging children into this baleful world. Nor would his desire to build a living monument to himself. Already there are more people alive than the Earth can support, and there is no point in creating new problems when we cannot even solve all of our old ones.

Death will solve all of our old problems. One by one, each of us will return to the nothingness whence he came. Being Itself is both our womb and our tomb. It's a pity that we ever had to leave It, but at least we can feel secure in the knowledge that we shall go back to It one day. When our time comes, all that we will have to do is give up and let go, and we will, because we will have to.

We shall be restored to Being Itself, but Being will not be fully restored to Itself until the last conscious being gives up the ghost and thereby brings the last part of the world to an end. That may never happen. Then again, it might.

In the last chapter, we noted that energy can neither be created nor destroyed—that it can only be transformed. This is the first law of thermodynamics.

The second law describes how, with each successive transformation, less energy remains for the performance of useful work. Whenever energy changes from one form into another (as from chemical to thermal energy in the process of digestion, from thermal to mechanical energy in an internal-combustion engine and from mechanical to electrical energy at a hydroelectric dam), we lose some of it forever. It turns into heat and radiates into its surroundings. This means that the energy available to drive our machines, to animate our bodies, to propel the planets in their orbits and to make the stars shine is steadily decreasing. The lost energy is not destroyed, but it can no longer be put to any use.

Heat moves naturally from a warmer area to a cooler one. This process is expected to go on until, as the last remaining form of energy, heat will be uniformly distributed throughout the universe. The absence of temperature differentials would make further energy transformations (including those necessary for life itself) infeasible. In this "heat death" of the world, as it is forecast by some physicists, all would be dark, formless and void—and no one would be around to see whether it was good or bad: All would be One.

This "heat death" is just a theory, mind you, based on certain assumptions that cannot be verified at present. Still, it's worth considering, and it's at least as plausible as some other end-of-the-world prophecies that involve angels on horseback, red dragons and monsters with seven heads apiece. Only time will tell which prediction, if any, is the correct one.

It will probably take a long time to find out—billions of years, perhaps. But no matter, the world has all the time in the world.

You and I won't have to wait so long. Each of us can look forward to his personal emancipation in the foreseeable future. As our lives flash before us in that last moment, each of us will be able to view life as little more than a bad dream that has disturbed the eternal sleep of nonexistence. And, when we are free at last, we can rest assured that what has cured our own ills will eventually cure all.

Someday, everyone will know it. The silence. And the peace … and the beautiful, beautiful end.

So, cheer up! After all, the best is yet to be.

Postscript

There are seven billion truths in the world. This has been one of them.

If You enjoyed this book
call, write or e-mail for a free catalog
Midnight Marquee
9721 Britinay Lane
Baltimore, MD 21234
410-665-1198
mmarquee@aol.com
www.midmar.com

www.ingramcontent.com/pod-product-compliance
Lightning Source LLC
Chambersburg PA
CBHW052148110526
44591CB00012B/1892